Teaching
From the
Deep
End

Second Edition

Teaching

From the

Deep
End

Second Edition

Succeeding
With Today's
Classroom
Challenges

Dominic Belmonte

Foreword by Gregory Michie

CORWIN
A SAGE Company

Copyright © 2009 by Corwin

For information:

Corwin
A SAGE Company
2455 Teller Road
Thousand Oaks, California 91320
(800) 233-9936
Fax: (800) 417-2466
www.corwinpress.com

SAGE Ltd.
1 Oliver's Yard
55 City Road
London EC1Y 1SP
United Kingdom

SAGE India Pvt. Ltd.
B 1/I 1 Mohan Cooperative
   Industrial Area
Mathura Road,
   New Delhi 110 044
India

SAGE Asia-Pacific Pte. Ltd.
33 Pekin Street #02-01
Far East Square
Singapore 048763

Printed in the United States of America

Library of Congress Cataloging-in-Publication Data

Belmonte, Dominic.
Teaching from the deep end: succeeding with today's classroom challenges/Dominic Belmonte.—2nd ed.
   p. cm.
Includes bibliographical references and index.
ISBN 978-1-4129-6561-3 (cloth)
ISBN 978-1-4129-6562-0 (pbk.)
   1. Teaching—United States. 2. Teachers—Training of—United States. I. Title.

LB1025.3.B455 2009
371.102—dc22   2009019903

This book is printed on acid-free paper.

09   10   11   12   13   10   9   8   7   6   5   4   3   2   1

Acquisitions Editor:	Carol Chambers Collins
Editorial Assistant:	Brett Ory
Production Editor:	Amy Schroller
Copy Editor:	Tomara Kafka
Typesetter:	C&M Digitals (P) Ltd.
Proofreader:	Eleni-Maria Georgiou
Indexer:	Judy Hunt
Cover Designer:	Scott Van Atta

Contents

Foreword

Gregory Michie

There's something about teaching and water metaphors. Preservice teachers are encouraged to get their feet wet by doing observations in classrooms. New teachers talk of treading water or of keeping their heads above it. And on their most difficult days, some teachers—even experienced ones—say they feel like they're drowning.

I know that last feeling well. I began my teaching career in Chicago with no formal preparation whatsoever, full of good intentions but with little else to guide me as I looked out at my first class of skeptical eighth graders. I spent most of my days that year teaching from the deep end. In fact, the pool I remember jumping into had no shallow waters—every end was deep. It was more like being adrift on a sea of surprises, challenges, and uncertainties.

If you've ever felt that way as a teacher—or if you think you might once you have a classroom of your own—Dom Belmonte tosses an invaluable lifeline with this book. Dom understands that the *whys* and *whens* and *whos* of teaching are just as important as the *hows,* and page after page he engages us in tackling the tough questions and thorny dilemmas. He avoids a prescriptive, by-the-numbers approach with writing that is passionate, wise, and witty (Imagine that—a sense of humor in a book for teachers!). All the while, he highlights the complex, never-finished work of figuring out who we are as teachers and what we value, encouraging us to face head-on the challenges of the profession while remaining always mindful of its amazing, life-changing possibilities.

I came to know Dom through his work with the Golden Apple Foundation, where he has spent nearly two decades helping guide hundreds of young people on the initial steps of their teaching journeys.

In the Golden Apple Scholars Summer Institute, a kind of summer camp for college students who plan to teach in schools of need, Dom and I often taught right down the hall from one another. Often I'd catch a glimpse of the eighteen- and nineteen-year-old scholars pouring into the hallway after Dom's class had ended, and I was always struck by their energy. Sometimes they'd continue hashing out a passionate debate on a hot-button issue. Other times, students would leave in a burst of smiles and laughter or with tears streaming down their faces. What I never saw was students coming out with a look of detachment or indifference. Dom urged them to engage, to reflect, to think, to care, to grow—both as teachers and as human beings. With this book, he invites us all to do the same.

Dom's lessons have staying power: His stories and reflections stay with you long after you've left his class—or put down the book. A couple years ago, I was having lunch in a downtown office with a group of Golden Apple Scholars who were by then teachers in class-rooms across Illinois. We started reminiscing about their experiences at Summer Institute, and one of them asked, "What do you remember most?" Without hesitation, one young teacher went up to a whiteboard, picked up a marker, and drew two perpendicular arrows meeting at a point. "That's what I remember most," he said. "I'll never forget that." Many of the other scholars nodded in recognition. I didn't understand the reference at the time, but it turns out it was a long-remembered lesson from Dom's class—one of many that he's included in this book.

If you're looking for ten easy steps to becoming a good teacher, you may want to look elsewhere. But if you're ready to be challenged, to rethink assumptions, to question yourself, to jump into the murky waters that necessarily accompany good teaching, then keep reading. You may not agree with Dom on everything—I don't—but that's part of the point. He's not looking for acolytes. He's here to help you find your own path as a teacher—your singular journey, as he calls it—and in that he is a most welcome guide.

Preface

I wrote what follows for my daughter, Mary Beth, and my son, Nic, so they could see.

I wrote what follows for the three people most responsible for helping me acquire the teaching passion: Bill Gorgo in high school with his knobby sweaters and scraggly beard and his movement from painting to album to poem to novel to sculpture to opera always asking, "See? See?" To the late Paul Carroll, a poet who spoke in the rain to angels and could hit consecutive three-point jumpers and pointed to the poem and asked me, "See? See?" And to the poet Mike Anania who encouraged and taught me how to question so my students could say, "Aha," as I asked, "See?"

I wrote what follows for my late father and the words we said in time and for teaching me what to value, how to hold.

I wrote what follows for my mother and her endless love and devotion to the always simple and right thing.

I wrote what follows for the great teachers I have worked with throughout my career, especially all who have worked at York Community High School in Elmhurst, Illinois, where from 1976–1996 I was patiently mentored then helped to patiently mentor a new generation of teachers.

I especially dedicate what follows in memory of my dear friend, Jerry Lombardo, who inspired a generation of students with his passion for music and his steadfast belief in the goodness of all children. He passed much too soon. As William Blake wrote, "We are put on earth a little space / So that we may learn to bear the beams of love." I mention him here with love and grief for a profound loss.

I wrote what follows to all the students I've helped and who've helped me. Thank you for the love and the laughter and the tears and the moments when we knew something special was unfolding.

I wrote what follows for all the students I've failed by my own word or deed. I remember each and every one of you and hope you're well and successful.

I wrote what follows for the Fellows of the Golden Apple Foundation and especially for Golden Apple's founders, Mike and Pat Koldyke. These two brave and generous people gave a teacher at the end of his career rope the belief that what he did and dreamed had merit. Bless them.

And I wrote what follows for my wife Mary Lee, for the life and ineffable strength her love has given me.

ACKNOWLEDGMENTS

I am grateful to Bill Ayers for being the first to read this manuscript, see value in it, and help it to find its audience by writing the foreword to the first edition. Bill is a rare and generous soul who continues to help others find meaning in their lives through teaching and who displays uncommon courage and tenacity.

I thank my colleagues: Nancy Northrip, Kathy Wandro, Penny Lundquist, Drew Bendelow, Peg Cain, Greg Michie, Dr. Penelope Peterson, Jim Pudlewski, who graciously illustrated this text, and especially Cissy Sullivan, whose comments touched my heart.

Most of all, I am grateful to my original editor, Faye Zucker of Corwin for her steadfast encouragement and gentle guidance of this manuscript past its original raucous stream of consciousness to something akin to rational thought. That this effort rests in your hands is due to Faye's deeply appreciated tenacity. For this second edition, I am grateful to Carol Collins and Brett Ory for encouraging me to expand upon what I began. I also deeply thank Tomara Kafka for finding the rough edges in my words to further polish but saw value within them anyway and said so. To touch the hearts of students in your sight is a blessing indeed—but to do so for those you do not see? Humbling.

PUBLISHER'S ACKNOWLEDGMENTS

Corwin thanks the following reviewers for their contributions to this work:

Melissa Albright
Sixth-Grade Communication Arts Teacher
Springfield R-XII School District
Springfield, MO

Michele Cheyne
Clinical Faculty, Science Teacher Education
University of Pittsburgh
Pittsburgh, PA

Kara Coglianese
Director of Learning
Wheeling School District 21
Wheeling, IL

Sara Coleman
Chemistry Instructor
Norwalk High School
Norwalk, IA

Carrice Cummins
Associate Professor
Louisiana Tech University
Ruston, LA

Sandra Moore
High School English Teacher
Coupeville High School
Coupeville, WA

About the Author

Dominic Belmonte taught at York Community High School in Elmhurst, Illinois, for twenty years as an English teacher and English Department chair. He now serves the Golden Apple Foundation for Excellence in Teaching as its president and chief executive officer. He was a Golden Apple Award recipient in 1987. In 1989, he co-created the Golden Apple Scholars of Illinois program, a pre-induction teacher preparation experience which is now Golden Apple's largest program. A 2001 study of the Scholars program conducted by the University of Illinois at Chicago proved participation in the Scholars program a significant factor in improving the preparedness of its participants. The John F. Kennedy School at Harvard University cited the Scholars program as one of fifteen programs out of 1,200 nationwide as a finalist for its Innovations in American Government award. In 1996, Dom also co-created the GATE (Golden Apple Teacher Education) program, an alternative pathway to teacher certification for midcareer adults wishing a career in teaching secondary math or science or elementary school children. He may be reached via e-mail at belmonte@goldenapple.org

PART I

Getting There

CHAPTER ONE

The Teaching Profession

What Are You Doing and Why Are You Doing It?

H ere are three truths about teaching:

1. There exists in this country a resilient core of spectacular teachers who deserve the title "teacher." Their very lives serve to instruct, energize, and inspire a generation of students.

2. There exists in this country another resilient core of teachers. This group does not inspire, does not teach well, and responds dismally to the challenge of educating children.

3. The educational community needs to find millions of new teachers who represent the first truth, and there is very little the educational community can do about those representing the second.

The United States faces a national challenge to improve our preparation of the next generation of teachers. We can hope to increase the likelihood that our children, especially children in urban, rural, and less advantaged school settings, can find themselves in the company of talented teachers. We know that consecutive experiences with teachers of quality can help children overcome the disadvantages of poverty. We also know the damaging effect a string of less than excellent teachers can have on the development of children.

We must acquire a new generation of quality teachers. We must do this in the face of a national perception of our profession as less desirable than other professions. We must do so in a nation that pays lip service to the importance of teaching but provides little in the way of incentives such as competitive salaries, professional working conditions, practitioner input on the development of curricula and school management, and clear professional advancement that does not take the quality teacher away from children. The irony of being a teacher is that we are often treated as children—forbidden to use a phone, required to ask permission to duplicate copies—teachers of twenty years' experience sadly realize they hold the identical responsibility as first-year teachers, and their expertise and experience generally are not sought to better their schools.

Despite these challenges, we must acquire this new generation of quality teachers. While legislators and pundits endlessly debate the many problems that we as teachers are not empowered to solve, we can still address one essential question central to quality teaching: How does one acquire the authority to stand in front of children as a teacher of substance and dimension? This authority does not derive from the power of the grade book or the crossly phrased word, and certainly it is not authority by demand. So how does one acquire the ability to become a great teacher?

I submit what follows as one path to the goal of quality teaching. It derives from the stuff and substance of a career in education, of learning how to teach, of reflection on improving my teaching, of imparting what I learned to others. It is based on the experiences I had in the classroom, as an administrator, and as the co-creator of two programs in Illinois that recruit and prepare teachers, one by presenting advanced teacher preparation for undergraduates (the Golden Apple Scholars of Illinois) and the other by offering an alternative pathway to teaching for midcareer adults. My quest as a teacher and as part of Golden Apple has been to advance the teaching profession. My goal is to see teaching perceived as a profession of honor that brings resilient and inspiring people into the lives of children who direly need resilience and inspiration.

How do we acquire a generation of quality teachers? Some misstate the process and call it teacher *training*. Dogs are trained. Teachers are prepared. Teacher preparation implies a journey, for becoming a teacher is a journey of thought and of action. A teacher must think about many things long before beginning to teach.

A teacher must reflect before doing and after doing. That sounds simplistic, yet there is preparatory work that allows a teacher to *do,* involving thought and structure.

I have always wanted to write about the ideas and themes of the courses I have presented to prospective teachers. It has been a singular honor to help create pathways to teaching for both undergraduates and mid-career adults. This desire to put down what I know and what I have done became even more acute when my daughter Mary Beth decided she wanted to teach high school English. It is certainly a unique feeling to have trod a certain path in one's professional life, then to glance behind to see your own child following it. While I am thrilled with her path, of course I worry for her as I worry for all who embark on this teaching journey.

We must provide a pathway to success for this new generation of quality teachers. We must work to raise perceptions about the value of the teaching profession in America. What follows is just as much for Mary Beth as it is for all of you who will read this book.

Three decades plus years in education has shown me that the process of becoming a teacher is very much the process of becoming a person. One grows into a stronger knowledge of what it means to be a teacher. One never finishes learning about how best to instruct and how best to inspire students. For those of you who wish to teach, for those of you who wish to inspire others to teach, for those of you young in the profession or those wanting to learn more—your time, by golly, has come.

Interpret what follows as steps along a path, one that must be approached with passion. You must enter the classroom with passion—not with some wild and unfocused enthusiasm, but with a passion formed by

- *Knowing* what you want to accomplish,
- *Seeing* those around you in order to begin properly,
- *Planning* to bring your students to knowledge and understanding,
- *Anticipating* challenges to that plan.

This passion cannot be manufactured. You know when someone is faking it up there by the big desk. The students can spot it even faster. No one wants to be that kind of teacher, not even those whose fatigue and cynicism have led them to fake it.

Think of it: the ineffective teacher does not arise this morning, look in the mirror, and say, "Today, I will be a perfectly horrid teacher. Today, I will hurt children. Today, I will take the path of least resistance. Today, I will dishonor this profession." No one looks in the mirror and thinks those things. Yet today, this moment, or tomorrow, across the nation, untold numbers of children are being poorly taught by unknown numbers of teachers. You know it's happening. How do such things happen?

Not to me, you may bluster. I will not be one of those teachers—the ones who perspire rather than inspire during their hour on the stage. Well and good. But how do you get to be good at this? How do you avoid becoming one of them?

So you must have passion, but your passion must be connected to a plan. The philosopher Immanuel Kant (2008) brought his study to three famous questions: "What can I know? What ought I to do? What may I hope?" The teaching passion involves three necessary questions you must always ask:

1. *What* are you doing?

2. *Why* are you doing it?

3. *How* can you improve how you do it?

Becoming proficient at answering the first two questions allows you to entertain the third. Having a clear knowledge of all three enables you to enter a classroom purposefully. That purpose directs you to package your knowledge and your plan in a compelling manner. That compelling manner gives you the necessary insight to look at your students. You thereby become a student of your students. That study allows you to proceed. But even before this thought is considered—you have to get a job! There is plan and structure even with that activity.

REFLECTIVE EXERCISE

For whom are you grateful? List those people and the gifts they have brought to you. Now examine that list. Does what you list define who you are? Is what you list reflected in your teaching?

Keep this list of gifts. What you list will in part define who you are, which will reflect how you teach.

CHAPTER TWO

Perception During the Job Search

How to Spot a School That Fits and One That Does Not

C hoosing your first assignment has some similarity to buying a car. You are unsure of the depth of detail to make a sound decision, you are easily swayed by your emotion in wanting one right away, you can easily be misled by what you don't see, and you may be blinded from seeing what's right there in front of you. Usually you are so focused on getting that job so you can relax and boast to your recently graduated friends that you have no worries that you ignore the warning signs until you find yourself in uncomfortable tension thinking there's something wrong here, or wrong with you, and is that feeling paranoia or normal?

Unlike past generations where American educators stayed in one spot for thirty or more years before retiring to the quaint ceremony and the awkward best wishes by younger colleagues and administrators, today's teachers expect to be more mobile and take the leap to other schools when they don't sense the support or the infrastructure. So you don't have to have the buyer's remorse night sweats wondering if you have bought a lemon. But it might help to have attuned antenna to sense the signs that the school you enter for an interview may be right for you. Here are some tips.

1. *First impressions are reality.* Those of us who enter hundreds of schools each year boast that we can sense a shaky ship soon after arrival and it's true. What you sense immediately upon entering are cues reasonable and oftentimes dead-on accurate. Surly security? Overwhelmed assistants? Messy hallways? Obnoxious and unrestrained student behavior? Like any business, you can tell if the workers there take pride in the impression they exude or are so full of ennui and stress that your presence there is seen as a bother and an afterthought. Good schools emanate their strength just as truly as weak schools exude their problems. Trust your senses here.

2. *Stop a teacher and a student in the hall and talk to them.* You're not trying to get the immediate skinny on the place from the student or the school's educational philosophy from the teacher. You're looking for impressions in their responses. Kids are unfailingly accurate in sifting through their emotions to be honest about their school. They'll wear their pride or insouciance on their sleeve for you to interpret. Teachers can put on a good face or choose you as their venting post in a quick denunciation of the place. Even an unprepared thought has meaning laden within it. Watch their eyes as they respond. The burnt out ones and the enthusiastic others will makes their impression known through direct statement or covert action.

3. *Ask the principal about the school's major challenge and how that challenge is being addressed.* Principals love to talk and may be taken momentarily aback by your question seemingly seeking the seams in the wallpaper. Confident principals articulate their problems. Ineffective ones sidestep the question and martinets deny any problems roil the school waters. A leader of a place that is on the upward trajectory admits its shortcomings—giving you the opportunity to express how you are part of the solution and not an aggravation of the problem.

4. *Seek out a custodial staff person for conversation.* Places that treat teachers poorly do likewise for their support staff. If you're strolling the halls with the principal and meet someone, you will not get the truest answer or impression—but if you're artful at detecting insincerity you'll get sufficient information from the exchange.

Don't get misled by trappings. A seemingly chaotic school could have the students' interests at heart as one with militaristic rigor and kids passing along as orderly as customers in those Visa commercials can be stifling. How are the people in that building regarded? In the walk-through and the conversation you can sense correctly if not blinded by fear of being without a job or wowed by the school's reputation.

Study the principal most of all—for the style emanating within that person sets the tone of the entire building. I recall being in a Chicago public junior high school that virtually sang with promise because of the strength and quality of the principal there. When that principal moved on replaced by the assistant, you could tell from the very air that something was amiss. Within three years, half of the staff left, the atmosphere surly and confrontational. Same kids—same address—but it was like night descended upon the school because of the limiting qualities of leadership. Don't discount this point one bit.

To paraphrase Yogi Berra, you can see a lot by looking. You're so confounded by anxiety and wired to impress and convince an administrator you're right for joining that faculty that you may overlook whether that place has sufficient structure to support and nurture you. So when the principal asks if you have any questions—fire away, not in a cocky sense or tone but as a student studying a subject. Here are a dozen questions worth asking:

1. As a new teacher mentoring is important to me. In what ways will I be mentored were I to work here?

2. Does the school employ scripted curriculum?

3. Is everyone supposed to be on the same page the same day?

4. What is the school's chief challenge and how are you addressing that challenge?

5. Is your door open for advice or should I see my direct report?

6. How do parents feel about entering the building and interacting with staff?

7. Who's the go-to person for advice and assistance?

8. How welcoming is the staff to new teachers?

9. How is the school's mission exemplified in its curriculum?

10. What was the school's historic approach to instruction and how have you exemplified or altered that approach?

11. Do you embrace shared decision making?

12. Is there a procedure wherein suggestions from staff are considered?

Again, here your instincts should be trusted. It is so—if you sense so, and taking a position somewhere to take a position may cause you more grief than passing on an offer for another. If you sense you can positively add to what you believe exists, it is the place. No place can be made better if your antenna gives you the warning twitch.

Of course, these impressions may not take until the fullness of time. You may be years away from truly knowing the tenor of your place. Principals can leave, the politics of the school may turn on its Machiavellian wheel and change things, the toxicity of your colleagues may be insurmountable. Remember—you are not consigned to be unhappy by choosing a school that does not fit. You cannot by yourself compel the faculty of a school with low morale to join arms and sing camp songs and rise together. You can try—you can exhaust yourself trying. But exhaustion is a funny thing—clouds your judgment, makes you error prone and susceptible to cynicism and soon, you're just like them! You cannot overcome the negative or condescending attitude of your superiors. But you can vote with your feet. You can choose from another of the thousands of schools each of our states hold and try again. Just remember your first job may not be your forever job and no teaching position contains an indentured servitude clause within the contract. There are kids who need you everywhere. If those in one building are in a place too corrosive for your spirit—seek another. The students in that building will be just as needy and quirky and marvelous as the ones you left. Worry not about the guilt of leaving. Someone took care of the little ones there before you arrived, and those that follow your leaving will be taught by someone—maybe not as well nor as passionately, but they won't be left on the street corner to freeze. You on the other hand will be in a place that nurtures and protects and provides opportunity for input. And that bounce in your step will echo in the concern in your voice. Your students will notice, and improve, and the crooked be straightened thereby.

REFLECTIVE EXERCISE

Task: Depict your school atmosphere, morale, perception of students and how you received those impressions. Revisit those thoughts multiple times during the school year to see if they have deepened or changed.

CHAPTER THREE

Your Educational Philosophy

Creating Your Teaching Tenets

Your longest pause as a teacher will follow reading the phrase found on employment applications new teachers fill out: *Describe your educational philosophy.* Quick—recite yours. Do you have one? You spent all that time in college reflecting about John Dewey. Meanwhile Johnny Dewey waits in your classroom, and he cannot read and may have dyslexia along with a dysfunctional home life, so how are you going to inspire Johnny? Quick—recite. This truly is the key to everything—why are you up there? What is your reason for teaching?

This is the challenge new teachers find soon after September hellos fade to the workaday world. Your reliance on worksheets and your struggles with uncomfortable silences and hesitations and ebbing confidence are all the result of too little reflection on the essential question: *Why are you up there?* You must have a reason. Your reason must connect to a belief system. You may be following a prescribed curriculum and that's fine. You may be forced to follow the pace of other teachers teaching the same subject or grade level and that's no sin. But *why are you up there?* This you have to figure out before you start working. Your belief system will drive why you teach what you teach. That belief system can segment the curriculum you plan to teach into units that are subsets of the tenets you hold dear. Every lesson and experience you offer your class that refers back to the unit theme should also cohere to the tenets you hold.

Your tenets create the *frame* of your teaching. They give your teaching purpose and meaning. Without purpose and meaning, you are marking time and time will become your enemy. Without purpose and meaning, classroom silences and the inevitable mischief that follows will be your students' recognition that you don't know why you're up there. With a frame, your teaching will be clear and focused. If you hold the frame dear, your students will recognize the substance you project, and they will follow along. You may struggle mightily with classroom management and mark rules on the blackboard and study systems of classroom management, for which quite a cottage industry has arisen. But consider this: *no classroom management technique can be more effective than a teacher who knows why he or she is standing up there.*

Your teaching tenets should fit on a single page. Two decades of reflection on the teaching profession brought me fifteen tenets. Everything I taught emanated from those phrases. I began all of my first classes, after the hearty hellos and the ever-traditional "Reading of the names," with this one-sheet explanation of "This is what you will learn in here." Each of these principles was created over years of errors and perceptions, reflection, and experience. And they all point to one principle from which these tenets stemmed:

The power of influence teachers wield is beyond perception. If you believe your students will achieve, they will, beyond their and your expectations. Limit their potential by what you hold in your mind about them, and you (not them, *you*) are responsible for that limitation.

I understand the arguments about students who come from disadvantaged homes or are the victims of poverty and impoverished parenting. *But the potential each child holds can blossom or wither depending on a teacher's decision.* Remember this well: any time you say, or hear another teacher say, "These kids can't . . ." or "These kids won't . . . ," what is really being said is "*I* can't," or more pathetically, "*I* won't."

You need to amass your teaching tenets and use them as the frame by which you present your lessons. Here are mine followed with expanded explanations for some of them:

FIFTEEN TEACHING TENETS

1. We are responsible for our actions. The consequences of our actions extend far beyond our ability to comprehend.

2. We are part of a legacy, and we can continue and improve that legacy.

3. If love is not the motivating factor in what you do, then why are you teaching?

4. Delay judgment. What seems often is not what is.

5. Making decisions when exhausted is unwise.

6. We will never fully master this art of learning and living. In struggling to approach mastery, however, we achieve dignity and honor.

7. We must hold command of our learning as strongly as our regard for children. One without the other damages.

8. By understanding and accepting ourselves, we come to know.

9. Any teacher provides a body of knowledge. A good teacher provides a way to hold that body of knowledge.

10. We teach what we are far more than we teach what we teach.

11. More lives have been touched and more lives have been saved in the space between a teacher's desk and a student's desk than have ever been touched or saved in any other space.

12. The path to students' minds often passes directly across their hearts.

13. In responsible and creative risk taking lies the beauty of accomplishment.

14. In what seems the most insignificant is often the most important.

15. In studying and trying to understand, we learn how to proceed.

WE ARE RESPONSIBLE FOR OUR ACTIONS

This is the seat of my teaching passion, one which hard lessons and witnessing the lives of adolescents over two decades has presented to me. In his novel *All the King's Men,* Robert Penn Warren (1996) wrote of "the web of things" that interconnects us and from which we are all affected by the decisions we make. That lesson was reflected in many of the literary works I presented to my classes.

In Ray Bradbury's short story "The Sound of Thunder" (1952) society has conquered time travel. For a fee, hunters could travel back in time to a point in history when a previously researched dinosaur was just about to expire so they could kill the extinct game. The time travelers stood upon a platform that hovered over the ancient ground, but they were ordered not to descend. One hunter does jump off the platform, however, and when the guides retrieve him and force him back to the platform, they note upon inspection that a butterfly lies crushed under the hunter's boot. They return to their present day to find in horror that everything has changed: a different language is spoken, and the democracy they left has been transformed into a totalitarian state.

Discussion about this short story would lead to the tenet. How could so much be changed by a circumstance so seemingly insignificant? The lesson became much more evident the year a student died in an alcohol-related car crash. The consequences radiated out to his friends and family and beyond—the wife that student never loved, the children he never created, the accomplishments left for others.

One year at the high school where I taught, my students and I researched alumni killed in battle to create a school memorial. The research brought us to Department of Defense records, amazingly detailed for victims of the Vietnam War, decreasingly so for Korea and the World Wars. A list of war casualties from the town newspapers brought our research group to the school vault to verify whether these deceased veterans were students who had attended our school.

We found that in the 1920s and 1930s student transcripts included photographs. My students were struck by the photos—the seemingly tough guy poses that served as a thin veil to adolescence.

They noted that honors students didn't seem to go to war. They noted that had those tough guys survived, their children might have been friends and classmates. They spoke about how those now dead must have wandered the same old hallways of our school, slamming the lockers with the same gusto on Fridays. They became reverential about these veterans and spoke about how their last moments must have been spent in pain, away from home and family. The lesson of what one poet called "the iron circumstance" burnt with those students of mine that week, and the tenet from which the lesson was crafted remains a pivotal understanding of life to me.

As a teacher, your responsibility for your actions is even keener. You must say and you must do up there, and what you say and do has profound implications, so profound that the meeker among us may just want to stand up there mute. You must say and you must do, however, for lives are in the balance. Think on that when you drag yourself into the building on a Monday morning, wishing to just shove worksheets in front of them for the day.

WE ARE PART OF A LEGACY

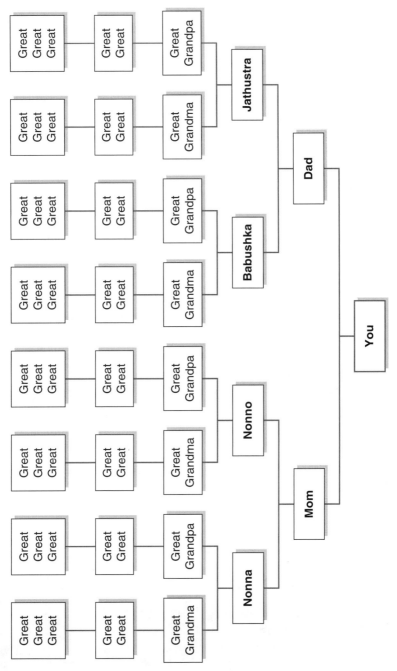

Very few of the students I have met can go far in this family-tree exercise. See how far you can go. For most of us, our memories peter out around the great-grandparent stage, even though those people, about whom we know little or nothing, carried our DNA strands and probably looked like us as well.

If any one of those on the diagram had a different fate, never had children or a spouse, you know the obvious consequence: no them, no you. One can surmise that they participated in a legacy of love and hope, that they loved their partner for a time and hoped their offspring would have a better life. In Thornton Wilder's play *Our Town* (1998) such a theme is presented. The narrator admits that all we know of the past is what may be on contracts or business records. But, he mused, people went home each night, smoke rose from the chimneys of homes, and the cycle of life continued unabated.

I believe this legacy of hope belongs to all our students. Even today, where our family trees have transplanted roots and hybrid limbs, students need to know that they can continue and strengthen their legacy. They can continue even if the circumstances of their family lives are not entirely happy.

The possibility looms that life will present a family tree like this to any one of us:

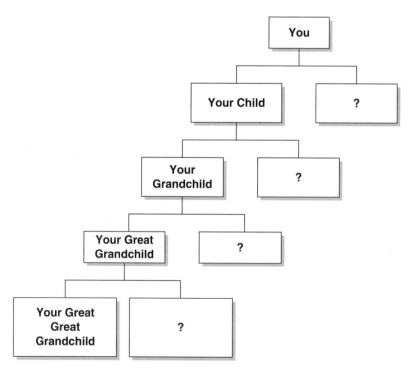

There will come a day when a great great grandchild of yours may know just as little about you as you did about the names that came before you, your mom, and your dad. But your great great grandchild may hope as you did that there was a legacy of love involved, that a partner was loved for a time and that there was hope for a child who might face a better life.

By such reflections are students shown that they are a part of something positive and lifelong. That is the teacher's legacy. In a world of broken promises and fractured families, we teachers can give our students the possibility that they will find the happiness and solace all of us seek.

After a career of teaching high school seniors, I looked forward to the end of the high school year: the nostalgia of spring, the baleful "senior stare," the inevitable distraction of signing yearbooks and saying goodbye. If you work as hard as you can to reach and inspire your students, it will not be easy to remove yourself from their lives. But that is the way it works, and so you do it with grace and a smile.

A few graduates may continue correspondence with you, but for the most part, two return trips usually does it for an alumnus. The first time they return is to show off their new hair style or facial hair or pierced adornment. The second visit brings to them a realization: How puny the place looks! The teachers are focused on their current students, and the returning students discover that what they seek— what helped them during their years in the building—resides within themselves and not within the building. So part of their growing up is putting behind that which made them young, including you. As their teacher, you must learn to accept that and you must help them accept that.

DELAY JUDGMENT

If I can impress only one thing that will help you become effective teachers, it will be *always remember to delay judgment*. The majority of teaching errors result from disregarding this tenet. Teachers too often judge incorrectly.

Scene: Student comes in without homework. But we want students to regard the homework we assign as important. We also want our students not to take advantage of us. So we lose patience. We lecture in front of all: "Homework is due when it's due. No exceptions." Fine. Wonderful. Order restored. Meanwhile, you discover later on that the student has spent the night in the emergency room with an ailing parent or has an otherwise legitimate circumstance. And you have lost the chance to acquire an ally. But your mania for an orderly atmosphere has certainly been enunciated. Bravo.

Students mask. What appears to be boredom is not, what appears to be disregard often is a cover for something else underlying. You cannot allow disrespectful behavior. But responding to a circumstance or a response or a vibe from a student in a thoughtless manner will often lead you to an incorrect assumption.

Scene: You encounter a student you believe may have plagiarized. In this case, attacking without a judgment delay always brings out heated denial. Whenever I had a premonition about plagiarism, I learned to call the student in during conference hour to talk about the paper. I asked the student how he or she arrived at the interpretations in the submitted paper. After a few sentences, the student who had plagiarized invariably stumbled. But in most cases, I discovered that students had not yet learned the necessity of citing their sources. They needed to learn how to blend their personal perceptions with published ideas in a manner that reflects intellectual honesty.

As a teacher you can gauge by the conversation how brazen or how innocent the appropriation was, then decide on a course of corrective action. Haranguing a student right from the start of the conversation may make you feel like the Righteous Angel of Intellectual Honesty, but you do not make the circumstance a learning experience by pouring on vehemence. In fact, instructors who speak with vehemence about students, whether individually or by group, have settled into a spasm of judgment that prevents them from truly seeing their students. It reduces their potential for success.

If you hear yourself say "These kids can't . . . ," always remember that translates to "*I* can't . . . ," and that is the opening phrase of your limiting your competence through inappropriate judgment.

MAKING DECISIONS
WHEN EXHAUSTED IS UNWISE

This is the advice our parents gave us about important decisions like buying a home or choosing a spouse. It is equally important in the teaching profession. Heed this carefully: Your measurement as a teacher will not be gauged by how well you do with the students who adore you. Anyone can benefit from interacting with such students. But the student who gets on your nerves, the dislikable student, the one who smells, the one who knows how to irritate you, the whining student, the argumentative student—your response to these students will determine your effectiveness as a teacher.

You will not even get the chance to gauge how successful you are with such a student on a good day, when the sun shines and the birds chirp. No, it will be when you have everything going south, your relationship awry, your parents ailing, your teeth hurting, the interruptions ceaseless, the day endless and unsuccessful—on that day, when that unpleasant student approaches you, will be your defining moment.

A cross-country coach I know liked to say his team was as strong as his weakest runner. So you are as strong as you are on your weakest day. If you decide to judge that student during that moment without thoughtful reflection, you'll discover your own limitations. A hard lesson brought this realization to me. Here is the story:

In my heyday as a teacher, it was five shows daily and I was having a ball. I was good and I knew I was good. We laughed and learned and I was full of myself. Students were conniving to get into my classes, and I accepted them because it was all part of the merry express. Showtime in the suburbs!

Such large classes gave me reams of papers to read, and I tore into them with relish sitting on the floor by the TV watching whatever. Some nights I would plop asleep right atop them. On one of those nights, I remember reading the first paragraph of a paper I assigned. I did not like how the first paragraph was structured. In those years, I was obsessive about first paragraphs: "Your first paragraphs are the map of the territory of the rest of your paper!" I would literally shout to the students. "Show an intriguing map, and your reader will follow into the territory of your paper."

This student's first paragraph wasn't going anywhere, and it was late. I circled the first paragraph, didn't read the rest, and jotted a note on the cover page asking the student to come see me for a conference. Then a few days later a student came to me with a transfer form. In the early parts of a term, students transfer in and out for all sorts of reasons—schedule changes in other classes, a desire to get out earlier for work opportunities. Since my classes were overcrowded anyway, I signed the note, wished the student well, and returned to teaching. Five shows daily! Showtime in the suburbs!

November came—time for parent-teacher conferences. In my heady heyday, I loved conference night. Other teachers dreaded that evening, but I reveled in the love fest: "You are such a wonderful teacher!" moms and dads would exclaim. "If I could be as good a parent as you, I would be grateful!" I exclaimed back. "You're great!" "You're great too!" Air kisses abounded. Affirmation overload.

But the last appointment I had that evening was a name I did not recognize. No matter, thought I, it could be a remarriage, or a parent road testing me for their child's appearance in my class the following year. A stocky gentleman in a mustache quietly sat down and looked at me.

"Do you remember _____," he asked me in a quiet voice.

"Uh, yes, I believe he was in my class for a short time." Quick look in my grade book. "Yes, for a week or so."

"Do you remember assigning him a paper?"

Another glance at my book. "Uh, yes, I see he was here for the first paper assignment I gave, but he dropped my class before a grade was recorded."

"Do you remember reading his paper?" He hadn't moved at all, just intently looking at me.

"Uh, I don't really recall. I read so many papers."

He handed me the paper. "Will you read it now?"

You know those moments in your career when the hairs on your neck fling up and corticotrophin, that substance that filters down your spinal column when you are frightened, begins its descent. Those are the moments when you know you are in the deep end, and I hope you never have too many of those moments, for the world really whirls and the bottom really drops.

So there was the first paragraph I had circled two months prior while exhausted in front of my TV watching whatever. This time I read the entire paper. And what I read was remarkably like the story line of Judith Guest's great novel *Ordinary People.* This young man wrote of his brother's death and his inability to accept it, his struggle with blaming himself for causing that death, his shame at having to live on while his parents wrestled with the loss of their more favored son. It was truly a remarkable reflection.

I forced myself to look up at this father, still not moving, now with tears running down his face. "My son has been in therapy since his brother's death. He has never been able to fully express how he felt—to his therapist, to us, no one." He now slowed to articulate each word. "This paper was the first time he put his complete thoughts into writing," he said, his voice rising, "and *this is how you responded to it?*"

What could be said? "Sorry . . . I was tired . . . sorry."

The father got up and left to relate his tale to the principal. And that was the year I won the Golden Apple Award for Excellence in Teaching. Five shows daily. Showtime in the suburbs.

On that evening all that hubris dissolved away. My lost opportunity weighed on me for weeks afterward. Fortunately for me, there was a positive resolution to this incident. I was allowed into the home of this family who received and accepted my abject apology. I championed the young man for bringing himself on the road to healing with no comfort or assistance provided by me to whom he had entrusted his pain. The father shook my hand as I left, but his eyes were unforgiving, and I thank him to this day for that lesson.

Like many teachers, I have a large envelope somewhere in my possession with all the nice things written to me by students and parents tucked inside it. I never throw away such words, although I never really reread them either. I daresay you may have such an envelope as well. On the front of my envelope, I have stapled the paper from the student who reached out to me whom I turned away in my blind and arrogant ignorance. Each time I file away another word of thanks or appreciation, that stapled paper reminds me that for every moment with every student I must never again make a decision based on distraction or exhaustion.

WE TEACH WHAT WE ARE FAR MORE THAN WE TEACH WHAT WE TEACH

Your very approach manifests what you are, what you value, and what you believe. The obverse is also true: If you reflect on nothing and stand for nothing and value nothing, then the vapid quality of your lessons will exhibit emptiness. A novice teacher may not know a plethora of instructional techniques, may not have strong subject matter grasp, or may not have a handle on understanding children. But all these can be developed if one has a set of tenets that define the reasons you wish to teach.

Remember your own favorite teacher. His or her lessons are only dimly recalled now, and the quizzes and tests are long forgotten. But you do recall the essence of that person. That excellent teacher's kindness or way of boosting your desire to learn is what you recollect. You retain what that teacher was to you. You may teach subject, but mostly you teach what you are, the way you animate the subject. Your essence is the contribution you make to the education of the children in your charge.

Bill Ayers, university scholar and distinguished professor in the College of Education at the University of Illinois at Chicago, is most eloquent and succinct on this point. Bill has long argued that the key to success in teaching is becoming a student of your students. The more you learn about them, the more you are able to intuit from careful observation and reflection on their words and actions who they are and why they are who they are. In their words and in their silences are the keys to understanding them. In their posture and in their manner are the cues you must learn to note. Try not to overlook possibilities that your students are communicating with you.

So too the underlying dynamic of the classroom offers your students the opportunity to observe you to gauge your effectiveness. They will watch your demeanor. They will tune in to signs of nervousness, of false bravado, of underlying personal problems affecting your mien. Your students may wildly misjudge how old you are, but they will be uncanny in their ability to perceive whether you are worthy of their attention and respect.

WHAT SEEMS THE MOST INSIGNIFICANT IS OFTEN THE MOST IMPORTANT

You will be continually surprised in your teaching at how the simplest of gestures and the most casual of circumstances can have the most profound effect on your students.

You may believe in the grand gesture and the dramatic pronouncements—I sure do. I wanted my classes to be anthems. I wanted to lead classes that had the same impact as Bruce Springsteen's early songs: powerful, complete, emotional, overwhelming. It was in my later years that I discovered the truly important and effective teachable moments were quieter: the encouragement written in the margin of a journal or the offhand remark that brightened a student's dour day. After years of practice, you become attuned to the possibility of such instances—teachable moments as they are commonly called, where the possibility exists that you can by decision or word choice profoundly change a student's opinion about himself or herself.

New teachers often miss these moments because they are focused so narrowly and so widely at the same time. New teachers worry about time, about following a lesson plan, about asking the prewritten questions, about whether or when the high-maintenance student will kick into need overdrive, all while the teachable moments pass without notice. And the trouble with traditional teacher preparation is that little attention is given to the perception of student cues in verbal and nonverbal communication. Anger, hope, doubt, disbelief, concern, apathy, arrogance—the entire array of adolescent human emotion can be seen in your classroom as in those Magic Eye pictures you have to stare at to see the hidden eagle or mountain range.

But if you enter the classroom with your own set of teaching tenets, then you will know where to look and what to do when you see the next teachable moment. If, for example, one of your tenets is "All students shall feel empowered in my class," then you will note signs of student apprehension as soon as they occur and you will be able to respond to them before they escalate. It's a bit like researching before buying a certain model car and suddenly seeing similar models on the road everywhere you drive. Having your own set of teaching tenets attunes your eye to what your students are emanating.

Make crafting your tenets your first priority. From your tenets will emerge the frame of your class, allowing you to create units that support and reveal the frame, allowing lessons to follow that will vivify those units. Having no tenets, struggle will ensue.

REFLECTIVE EXERCISES

1. Your Legacy

With today's technology, we have advantages our ancestors did not. We can record our image, our words, our thoughts. Record yours: What would you say to your future children's children yet unborn? What would you wish to hear them say to you?

2. Your Teaching Tenets

Revisit the statement you created at the end of Chapter 2 about the one thing always true in your classroom. Try placing that statement at the top of your list of teaching tenets. What other tenets should you have? Allow this list to keep expanding as you continue in this profession.

CHAPTER FOUR

Reflective Writing Exercises for New and Veteran Teachers

W hen preparing new teachers, I always insist that the keys to their success will be found in knowing themselves, in knowing which tenets they wish to project to their students, and in knowing why they believe those tenets are so important. Students see their teachers as survivors of challenges both academic and personal. They look to their teachers for direction, and they gauge whether the promise of that teacher is dimensional or limited. Students dismiss teachers with specious beliefs about power. And they dismiss teachers who demand respect rather than command it. Teachers who have a grasp of their own lives, who have reflected on what has occurred and how it has shaped their persona, are able to succeed. They are more comfortable in their own skin, know who they are, and reflect to students a confidence and assurance that offers students direction. The path toward the challenges of adulthood seems safer and more plausible to students when they see someone successful standing at the head of their classrooms.

Students will naturally gravitate toward adults who offer them a hope that life, with all its burdens, offers reward as well.

"The unexamined life is the life unlived." In reflection and in examination of the teaching life, each one of us can find the reason why we wish to teach.

Here is a selection of preparatory exercises that will allow you to determine who you are, why you are who you are, what it is you may project to students, and what value you may bring to your work with students.

THE ADHESIVE MOMENT

Memory is such a powerful experience. The conduits of memory span stimuli: a smell, a sight, a song, a place, an anniversary, a fabric. Adhesive memories are forged not only by trauma and events of significant impact, but also by the quieter moments whose significance grows as years intervene. This exercise asks you to search your memory with attention to detail.

Think back across your life. You've forgotten many things about your school years, I warrant, but recall a moment when a teacher hurt you by word or deed. I will predict that you can recall just about everything, chapter and verse. Here's mine:

I grew up in the Little Italy West Side of Chicago in a two-flat with a cartage company in the basement run by my uncles. I recall with clarity telling my fourth-grade teacher Sister Mary Perpetual Astonishment (name changed, of course) that I wanted to teach someday. It was a cloudy day. I wore a white shirt with a blue clip-on tie. She told me, "With your family history, dear, your best hope will be to work with your uncles on their trucks."

Now I know there is absolutely no dishonor in the trucking profession. My point is that my teacher told me that I could not become what I wanted to become, and that memory remains to this day. As teachers, how many children do we damage by adding to their memories something that limits their potential, dams their spirit, clouds their skies?

So the assignment is to recount a memory (that you are comfortable recounting) that holds a certain adhesion to your mind. Why do you think it remains? The adhesive moment exercise brings a relevance that reveals, especially through the passage of time, an understanding of self. In studying and in trying to understand, as one of my own teaching tenets suggests, we can learn how to proceed.

How will you respond to receiving such a personal writing effort from a student? Surely you won't begin with the grammar or narrative structure, although that will have a place at some point. Rather, I hope you will hail the passage that has occurred through reflection. Will you thank the writer for trusting you with a part of what has made her who she is? Will you wonder at this profession where you have had the opportunity to be a healer, to witness the conduit between what students bring into your classroom and what they leave with?

Remember: you can heal and you can harm. Or you can do so little as to be undetected as they pass through your class on their pathway to somewhere else.

TRACKING MY BIAS

Remember that your effectiveness as a teacher will not be gauged by how you work with the students who love you or who make your days run smoothly. Those who trouble you, who make your days dark and confused, who confound you, those are the students who will define your effectiveness as a teacher. Moreover, the students most unlike you and most unlike your image of what students should be like, those will be the students who will gauge your talent. Those students will rub against your biases. Let's all take a moment to protest that we love all children and we harbor no biases. Let's exclaim until weary, and then we can think again.

S. I. Hayakawa presented a brilliantly simple theory of how bias is acquired in his work *Language in Thought and Action* (1949/1991). Hayakawa termed it the action of "the little man who isn't there." By those we love and admire or by circumstances in our lives, we acquire in our heads a map of the people who represent the groups for whom we harbor bias.

So many of us recognize the false map that shows the Italians who treat women as objects, the Irish who are drunken romantics or power-mad politicos, the Asians who are overzealous curve-busters. In the context of the high school, the false maps are further delineated. Therein the thespian is the over-dramatic homosexual, the athlete dull and vulgar, the pom-pom student callous and materialistic. And, of course, the faculty is clueless and sad without a scintilla of heart or humanity.

On and on the maps are drawn. So when one "sees" someone representing a group one holds in bias, according to Hayakawa (1949/1991), that person is not truly seen. What is seen instead is "the little man who isn't there," which strips the person in front of us of identity and individuality. So our false maps prevent us from seeing the brilliant athletes, the coarse academics, the cheerleaders of great merit and worth, the auto mechanics with poetic understanding and appreciation of the components of things. But unless and until we rewrite our false maps, we will be denied knowledge of such real persons and banished from real understanding, left to wallow forever in the idiocy of our superficial perceptions of "those people" who behave "that way."

How much waste holding such maps! We who teach must recognize our own false maps, take stock of how we acquired our biases, and study what we are doing to efface those biases. The teacher with biases who stands in front of students will make those biases as visible as the harvest moon in October.

Prospective teachers find this a difficult reflective exercise because it takes one outside the realm of nostalgia and symbol into the real and the difficult. I used to call this exercise "Why I Hate: What I Must Do," but I changed the title to "Tracking My Bias" after students and prospective teachers claimed they did not really hate anyone or anything. Perhaps hate does escape some, but bias tinges us all. Students and prospective teachers who have undertaken this reflective exercise have written about every ethnic group and some stereotypes as well. One wrote about his distaste for blonde women; many women write about their disgust with men. All say their efforts with their biases are a work in progress, and that is the best that we who prepare future teachers can hope to achieve.

The reason bias proliferates is that we are not prone to place ourselves in positions of actually looking at each other as people. It is far simpler to categorize and assume than it is to individualize and discover.

Watch how tempted you will be to fall on your preconceptions and false map biases in the classrooms. The teaching task is so exhausting, the demands so relentless that temptation will rise merely from your weariness. The moment you allow your biases to surface, your students will notice it. Students are more attuned to that part of your mien than any other aspect of your teaching. They take for granted your subject matter mastery. They will give you license to falter in your class structure on occasion. They will be quiet when they sense you need them to be (unless you have lost their regard, for then they will revel in your confusion). But demonstrate bias and nothing can camouflage your bias.

It is vital that you examine "the little men who [aren't] there" in your mind. We all must recognize our false maps, take stock of how we acquired our biases, and study what we are doing to efface those biases.

THE AUTOBIOGRAPHICAL FAIRY TALE

As a young teacher, I experimented with ways to get students to open up, to abandon the artificial selves so many don in an attempt to move away from serious reflection. The comfortable, structure-laden "In my paper, I will compare basketball to football" formulaic paragraphs that pretend to be essays are the comfortable refuge of many students. I hoped to convince them that their writing assignments were photographs of the interior of their minds and hearts. While most photographs of ourselves make us cringe, with practice we acquire an understanding of our true selves. I sought to move beyond the stock and the blurry in essay assignments.

One early successful project focused on the fairy tale. We read tales from the Brothers Grimm and Mother Goose in an effort to see how moral was embedded in the tale. Then I asked them to write a fairy tale that would impart a lesson they would wish their children to learn. So they would start in reverse order, crafting morals that meant something to them then animate their morals with fables they'd create. What would surface were essays on the nature of Tommy the Goldfish, who was your average ordinary goldfish living well in his goldfish world with his friends happily until the day Tod showed up. Tod was a goldfish that looked different—a ripped fin, a different hue. The other goldfish were suspicious of Tod and didn't want him playing their goldfish games. Then came the day when Tommy got to see Tod's true nature. He was just like the other goldfish. Tommy told his friends to back off. Tod was cool, and all remained well in the goldfish world.

Such assignments were done well enough. The students offered a glimpse of their values and activated them by symbolic manipulation of the structures inherent in fairy tales. But the assignment did not approach what I sought.

About this time my own children were young and of the age to hear stories. My forays into the library for bedtime reading material brought me to a realization of how today's society is reflected in children's literature. Looking for variations of "Rapunzel" or "The Fox and the Grapes" brought me to titles such as "Daddy Doesn't Live Here Anymore" and other announcements of the scary new order. On one of these library hunts, I happened upon Bruno Bettleheim's work *The Uses of Enchantment* (1975). Bettleheim's writing and life work has spiraled into neglect after allegations about him surfaced after his death. His psychological interpretations of traditional fairy tales were also rebuffed in his time. So it was in amusement that I read his theory of Rapunzel, the story of a girl locked in a tower by a fearful parent to prevent her from meeting suitors. The plan was repelled by Rapunzel, who grew her hair long enough to allow her suitor to climb up the tower to her aid. Bettleheim felt this was the tale of a young woman whose parents vainly attempted to stop their daughter from reaching sexual maturity. Such an attempt is futile, Bettleheim urged, because children know instinctively such attempts are wrong and should be repelled, for no person can prevent another from achieving his or her destiny as a sexually active person.

Bettleheim theorized that traditional fairy tales embedded problems within them, involving children otherwise left to their own devices to solve. With the help of the wise owl or the babbling brook, such answers were provided. Children who like a particular tale, Bettleheim wrote, did so because the imbedded problem in the tale matched the problem they unconsciously recognized existing in their own lives and through the retelling of such a tale sought resolution.

Now I had trouble thinking that my daughter, when she asked me to reread "Rapunzel," was plotting her rebellion. But reading his work brought me to rethink the fairy tale as a conduit for reflection. The genre uses symbol manipulation that can allow one's values to surface. Using symbol manipulation in writing reflectively would allow students to write their feelings camouflaged in a symbol system they could easily interpret. From these thoughts was borne perhaps the most successful writing assignment I ever used with students: write the story of your life as if it were a fairy tale. Giving students the authority to select the moments of their lives they wish to convey and the freedom to create a symbol system that would animate the people and events in their chosen moments gave them a great freedom. They could write with passion and clarity cloaked in the fairy tale world they could understand.

The quality of the writing I receive from such an exercise is almost always stunning. They also were oftentimes difficult to interpret, since the author holds the key to understanding each particle of the fairy tale world created and the meaning imbedded within it. But I found myself not caring if I understood every nuance. What was important was their reflecting, and by such reflecting learning how to proceed.

One student of mine was particularly opaque in her reflective written work. Her interpretive skills with literature were excellent yet early personal reflections offered little. In introspective writing, it was essential for me to inform my students that they controlled the boat they rowed. Nothing that made them uncomfortable reflecting needed to be forced out. All moments take time to digest, and the meaning of those moments comes in revelation in slow degrees as the years pass the veils of introspection over them. I forced no skeleton shaking through the assignments I gave. Then I assigned the autobiographical fairy tale.

I have already told you about moments in your career when you will be blown away by the work of your students. Years later, rereading what Nina wrote still sends chills through me. In terms of its understanding of self and of that time in her life, its clarity and insight stuns. Seeing such power in the writing of an eleventh-grade student brought me to always believe in the ability of young people to reflect upon the circumstances of their lives and seek through that understanding a pathway to continuing.

All one needs to know in glimpsing Nina's tale is that the oak tree represents high school and all the caterpillars upon it students.

A Tale

by Nina Smithe

Well then, my child, you tell me you are unhappy, you, who continually grasp for things beyond your reach, not realizing that they are unattainable and, if stripped of their glittery façade, undesirable. You, curiously afraid of others and wishing with all your might to rise above them, as if they were something detestable, alienating yourself behind a wall of perfection. Let me tell you a story, and listen carefully to what I say, child, before it is too late for you as it is now too late for me.

(Continued)

(Continued)

Several years ago in a small garden near the gnarled roots of an oak tree, a colony of caterpillars lived. The tree was only a temporary stopping point though, until they acquired their strong, splendid wings, which would enable them to venture into the sky. The caterpillars often dreamed of their future, but for now they were content with their simple lives and enjoyed crawling in mud and among the blades of grass.

However, one caterpillar (how much reminiscent of you) would struggle to the topmost branches of the oak and gaze longingly at the birds and butterflies, craving to join them as they freely soared through the air yet, at the same time, wanting desperately to belong to the group of caterpillars on the ground. She was somehow a little different and the other caterpillars sensed this and rarely approached her. Perhaps her thoughts and dreams were so much more extreme and painful that she was no longer a part of their world. Her loneliness, though, was partly her fault, for whether due to weakness or fear, she rarely attempted to climb down from the lofty branches and speak with the others.

Perhaps she hadn't meant to form it, but nevertheless, a cocoon gradually built up around her, layer by layer, until it was almost impenetrable. There she nestled, snugly enveloped in an illusion of warmth and love, sheltered from the cold air and quizzical, harsh stares of the others. Inside her cocoon, she planned and dreamed and fastidiously selected her beautiful colors, carefully rearranging them, attempting to find the pattern that best suited her. When she would finally emerge, she would dazzle the world with her radiant magnificence, soaring above the heads of the common caterpillars, who would look up in awe at her beauty and feebly reach out to her.

Sometimes, making a special effort, a few of the caterpillar's old friends would struggle up the tree to her cocoon and try to coax her out. But she would always decline, being completely absorbed in her plans. She would tell herself that she had no need of love, especially from the ignorant little caterpillars on the ground. But she was mistaken, for inside she craved it more than anything else. Perhaps she imagined she could only find happiness by attaining perfection. She was oblivious to the fact that this was the very thing that drove it away. Isolated in her lofty tree, the cocoon imperceptibly began to harden, and with it, so did the caterpillar's emotions and ability to care and love. But still she continued her vain pursuit of unattainable beauty, loathing her own imperfections as well as the blemishes of the other caterpillars, which were easily perceived when they tried to come close to her.

Meanwhile, the rest of the colony squirmed among the roots of the oak tree out in the sun. Unsheltered by cocoons, they were often cut as they crawled about, but these scratches soon healed and were replaced by stronger, wiser fibers through their exploits. They discovered which leaves were delicious and which ones would make them sick. And, most important of all, they learned to laugh at, and eventually love, their own ugliness.

One day a small tree animal, perhaps hungry or simply unaware of all the elaborate dreams encased in the cocoon, gingerly picked it up between its front teeth, chewed it, and sent it sliding down its throat into a vitriolic pool of stomach acids. The other caterpillars were shocked and a little saddened by this occurrence, but in time, these feelings passed and she was forgotten. What is one dead caterpillar out of the millions that inhabit the earth? And she had never been a very friendly caterpillar anyway.

So, my child, you ask what happened to the other caterpillars? Well, a few always remained in their earth-bound forms, but most, without any special planning or sacrifice, eventually blossomed into colorfully winged butterflies, although a little less dazzling than the lonely caterpillar's ideal.

Think carefully about what I have told you. You must help yourself, child, no one else can—least of all me. For I can shed no tears over your misfortunes nor smile at your triumphs. My heart is encased in an iron cocoon that I, in my folly, put there by myself.

Author's Note: The author wishes to thank the essayist for permission to reprint "A Tale." The essay originally appeared in *The Journal of the Illinois Council for the Gifted* (1990).

When you establish an atmosphere of trust and responsible risk taking, using a framework for your lessons that hearkens back to a set of tenets you hold as essential to your reason to teach, then the possibility emerges that you will be seen as an instructor worth focused attention. The results can be effort from your students that far exceeds expectation. You show them the reflection of your tenets, and they reflect back their growing sense of understanding, through your work, of who they are and what they must do to continue growing.

I encourage you to try this reflective exercise yourself. The act of selecting moments and assigning symbols to them, and the manner in which you manipulate them, will speak clearly about your pathway heretofore.

Why do so? How can you begin to approach an understanding of your students without an understanding of yourself? How will you recognize their struggle for becoming if they cannot see you as someone who has undergone that struggle? That you have survived personal and professional challenges will influence them. They will understand the necessary discipline of your study as they see you as worthy of trust and emulation. Teachers of limited ability actively decline to act upon set tenets. They respond to reactionary assumptions about students and act in a manner that will produce the limited results teachers believe exist in their students. They do not trust students to push themselves to greater levels of achievement. Because these teachers will not, their students can not.

Is that the legacy you wish to continue? If not, get busy knowing thyself and learning where you need to go to develop as a teacher of dimension and substance to your students.

TEACHING AS SONG: PUTTING YOUR REASONS FOR TEACHING INTO A LYRIC

Our teaching lives are a type of song, sung in a place where others witness. If you sing with readiness and with spirit, your classroom can become a place of order, where one may find a deepened sense of what it means to be human.

For many years, I have asked students and prospective teachers to write songs and sing them to their peers. That seems to me to be a distillation of the teaching challenge: to allow themselves to be open, to be seen and heard, to send forth from their mouths a voice that through spirit attempts to bring order to their world. I asked them to write songs about why they wanted to teach; what about teaching compelled them to study further.

The act of singing their songs has always been a gracious, cathartic event. In those venues, we did not care about the quality of one's voice, for we are all in the process of perfecting our voices as teachers and as people. I conclude this chapter with the lyrics of a past prospective teacher. I invite you to consider and craft your own song. This you will be doing during the entire extent of your life as a teacher.

The Lesson

by Laura Cottrell

Are you ready to teach?
Why are you playing around?
It's a serious profession,
Don't need promises that fall to the ground.
Are you ready to teach
With its responsibilities?
Don't know the meaning of scholar,
Can't get by with inactivity.

You say you don't need direction,
That you've figured it out,
But if you listen to wisdom,
You'll succeed, no doubt.
Are you ready to teach
With all your negativity?
I hope you change your position
To ignite your inner beauty.
They say that life is a circle
And what you sow you shall reap,
Well if you try to play your teachers now
What makes you think your turn will be sweet?
I'm not trying to preach
But are you really ready to teach?

I hope so much for you to succeed. You will learn that the children indeed do call. Yet the call is muted, disguised in pose and bravura, camouflaged by unconcern and apathy. So much damage may have already been done to their creativity and their capacity to believe in themselves by the teachers in their past that by the time you meet them, they may already have written you off. Disappointment may have led them to anticipate that you too will falter, give up on them, sell them short, or walk away. Disappointment may increase their cynical belief that school is useless outside the curricula of the hallways. But their very reticence is a call for you to act. Their insolence is a call for you to proceed with intelligence and meaning. Their silence is a call for you to demonstrate that their lives do have meaning.

Start by walking into your own classroom resolved that you will not give up on a single child. You may enter your classroom thinking, "If only they will move halfway, I will meet them." They are looking at you thinking, "If only this one can show some care and move halfway toward me, I will approach." You have only to move with a plan and an attuned ear, staunch belief, and resilience. Your efforts will be rewarded many times.

I started this book by asking you if you think you will be ready. No one ever really is totally ready for the immensity and the complexity of teaching. But you can increase the odds for success. Have a plan. Have a reason to stand up in front of your students. Let your every action be based on a tenet. Listen to them. Learn from them. You can and will find moments in your classroom when you are absolutely sure you are saving lives and healing wounds. You can almost hear it when it happens.

When you do hear, when you do see, you will be ready.

Acknowledgments: The author thanks Nina Smithe (pseudonym at former student's request) and Laura Cottrell for permission to reprint their reflections.

CHAPTER FIVE

Remember the
Paul Potts Principle

It Is So (If You Think So)

The power you can generate as a teacher must never be under-estimated. While you work under the gaze of your students, you are being judged, and you, whether you know it or not, are judging them, and they seek signs in your demeanor that indicate your perception. A common teachers' malady is students complaining of "favorites." When the charge is leveled your way, you will think, "No way! I treat all my students the same." Yet do you? How that impression becomes registered in students' minds and promulgated to the community of your classroom is part of the mystery of interpretation of gestures, stance, comment, gaze, position in the classroom that students seem to note with such eerily sensitive regard. You think you are just conducting a class, moving about its components, hoping that the time passes without incident; yet the time passes replete with incidents, students coming in and out of their respective musings to focus with uncanny precision on the subtextual nuances of your mien. In their focus, they ask more basic questions than the ones associated with your topic of the day. In their focus, they judge: Is this person worth my time? Is there competence on display here? Is this person a jerk, a hypocrite or a joke? In their focus they judge themselves by the vibe they think you evince: Does this teacher think I'm a loser? Am I seen? In their focus they consider inferences: Look at these suck-ups trying to brownnose their way to a grade. This teacher can't be more obvious. Or the worst of judgments they can bestow upon you through their focus: This is so damn boring! What will I do about my job? Why are Mom and Dad always angry? Where will we party this weekend? They escape into the reverie of their internal curriculum as a respite from their perceptions of your perceptions.

Return to your own life as a student and reflect. Did you not engage in such mental practices? Were you not ever seen in your own eye as the outcast or the favorite in the classroom? Did you practice being so hidden that your teacher seemed to place a shroud of invisibility around you? And did you not judge as ye believed ye were judged? How many teachers had you written off in your student career? How many did you believe wrote you off?

From where do these impressions come? The mind does them instinctively, racing to order the otherwise chaotic that occurs in front of us. The mind seeks order and rationalizes through inference what exists in our visual field. S. I. Hayakawa (1949/1991) in *Language in Thought and Action* defined inference simply as "a statement of the unknown made from the known." We use this concept all the time. You see a friend with dark circles under her eyes and assume what? Lack of sleep, illness, perhaps a problem nags. You sit in your car at a stoplight in the city and your hand reaches out to the door lock when you see someone you depict as disheveled, dangerous, or frightening approach. You yell at your significant other, who responds, "I did not say anything!" and you say, "But you have that look!" meaning you have interpreted meaning (the unknown) through their facial expressions (the known). There are legions of parents who look upon their children's friends with the inference portion of their brains ablaze with criticisms that, while seemingly based in truth ("That one looks like trouble." "She's a druggie." "He's going to take advantage of our little girl!") are based on supposition and assumption. This ability to use our insight is often very valuable in reading situations and people, but the ability is not foolproof. Oftentimes, in the heat of moment or circumstance or when distracted or tired, our inferential motor misreads and misfires.

The misfiring in the classroom takes many forms. Young teachers often misread and overact to management circumstances by inferring more into situations than is there. Wandering interest in subject is not automatically a sign of disrespect. Your perceptual acuity of your students can be based on inaccurate (or worse, biased) inferences. So the student who does not pass your filter as prototypical (hygienic, coiffed, clothed, and at the very least odor-free) may unnecessarily fall into your perception in a less than positive frame. From such erroneous suppositions come others. You doubt the veracity of work. You sense disruption at every gesture. You build in your mind a case for classifying such a student into a place he or she does not belong.

Then the amazing happens—the student then becomes what you believe him or her to be. You may congratulate yourself on your powers of ratiocination. But what has really occurred is *not* that you have accurately pegged your student. Actually, the student has perceived the timbre of your disapproving perception of him or her, and then consciously altered behavior to match your perception. Congratulations, Dr. Frankenstein! You have made what you have thought, and not successfully depicted what you thought you saw!

The Italian absurdist playwright Luigi Pirandello titled one of his works "It IS So (If You Think So)," which is to me an apt epigram for this tendency of teachers to misread students, act upon that misperception, and have students ape that impression due to their superior inferential powers. I name this tendency the Paul Potts Principle after a rather thrilling moment in the history of reality television.

To see it yourself, find "Britain's Got Talent Paul Potts 1st Audition" or a version thereof on YouTube. The more recent version, which seemed to attract so much more attention, occurred with Susan Boyle's appearance on the same show in 2009. "Britain's Got Talent" is the original version of what appears in the United States as "American Idol" so you have a sense of the circumstance. You see a sizeable young man with uneven teeth speaking about his desire to sing opera. He walks onto the stage and the three judges pass ominous looks to each other. The eponymous Simon Cowell asks what Paul wishes to sing, and when he replies, Opera," you can read the looks on the judges' faces (in itself an inference!) as anticipating disaster. Eyes rolled, deep breaths taken, face twisted. They brace themselves for the kind of disaster shows of this kind ordinarily like to trumpet in some macabre celebration of human frailty. Then Paul starts singing the difficult and evocative "Nessun Dorma" from *Turandot.* I have written about that aria before, with its mystical ability to draw emotion out of people. Look at the look on everyone's faces as Paul sings—certainly not to the quality of Pavarotti—but superbly. The power of Paul's passion and the power of music overcame the inferential presumption of the judges and audience that they had a doofus in front of them worthy of their scorn when they were moved to tears by his performance.

Paul Potts and Susan Boyle are metaphors for all the students you have who tempt you to categorize because they do not come to you as you perceive students to be—the ones with weight challenges and in need of dentistry, the awkward and the gangly and the isolated, shy and forlorn. The audience knew a chubby mobile phone salesman or a dowdy schoolmarm looking woman was in front of them and assumed they would have a moment where they could chortle and mock and instead stood on their feet moved by the power of music and lyric and passion. It was a moment of triumph you could help engender in your classroom if you would delay your judgment and belay your inference and see just the nascent talent in front of you and help it to surface. Notice in the film clip the words of praise the judges give him and watch Paul's face as he hears such praise. You witness the balm such words have on the heart. Who knows what inner qualities exist inside your students? Learn them and celebrate the Pauls and Susans you will teach as much as the ones you have who seem to have it all together.

I well remember a student I had who was pilloried by his classmates for his gawky, geeky behavior. He played violin (and why are such musicians targeted for such teasing?). He did have some unique quirks—especially the tendency to twist his arms about his body and turn his head into the crook of his elbow as if he were, as the poet Ed Dorn wrote, "an angel flying into myself." Sometimes I had to stop myself from staring at him do his dance to himself. Sometimes I shouted out a "C'mon, quit that!" when it got to be too much a distraction.

Bus rides were the worst thing for him, when the teasing would be brutal. In his journal, he referred to all those who made fun of him as the "wildebeests" and never wrote one word of recrimination about them.

I never really knew my contribution to this student's life. I protected him from scorn and derision in my class, graded his work, and complimented him when his writing made sense.

Years later, when I got a congratulations/thank you card from this student, with his title as "Chief of Surgery" at a Midwestern hospital, did I realize I had had a Paul Potts in my midst. Did I help?

Maybe not much—but I know I did not allow him any harm while he was in my sight—and that's a good enough cautionary tale for you to keep a sharp eye on the cruelty amongst the students in your classroom and their targets.

REFLECTIVE EXERCISE

Keep a journal on one or two of your students throughout the course of the school year. Choose two with some kind of distinguishing differences—both problematic but in different ways, one a challenge and one a teacher's dream of a great student, one male one female, one an athlete one an academe. How does your relationship evolve with each? What do you try? How did it turn out? Case studies give you the opportunity to engage in reflective practice.

Part II

Being There

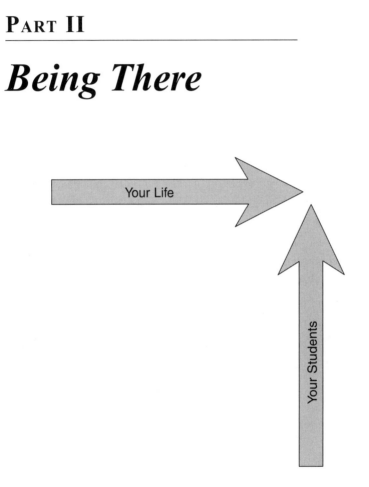

Your Life

Your Students

CHAPTER SIX

The Classroom

Where the Teacher's Path and Student's Path Converge

Turn to the preceding page and look again at those arrows. Think of them as an approximation, like all images, of the reality you may have experienced on your pathway to becoming a teacher. One line represents your life. Of course its path has not been arrow straight. The moments of your life that have defined you take years of reflection to unravel. Your learning, your reading and writing, the steps you took to acquire the intelligence you command, the person you are, none of these can be so easily represented. Yet pretend for a moment that one straight arrow can represent your path through life. You've come from a direction, traveled a path to where you are right now, holding this book, and moving onward. Congratulations! You have made it this far on your journey, as wonder and hope drive you onward into the mystery of what's ahead.

The other arrow represents the pathways of the students you will meet, young people from different lives who have experienced different moments and have acquired different knowledge from those moments. All those youngsters, and all their moments, have gathered by fate and circumstance in the classroom you now or will soon sit in, and they will be waiting. Your separate lives have converged in this one place for an appointed time. When they enter the classroom and sit and look at you, then you will understand the image on the preceding page and its significance.

Will You Be Ready to Teach?

You have studied and you have learned. Your methodology class lurks somewhere nearby in your mind, but the theory you studied becomes the theory forgotten as the students now look at you with wondering, weighing eyes. Now you understand that you're in there for a reason. You wanted to do this, always wanted to be up front, in charge, and you believed being by the big desk put you up front and in charge. You know they are looking and you know they are weighing and so you must begin somewhere and somehow. Will you be ready?

There may come a time when one of them will die in circumstances tragic or senseless, and there will be one empty desk in a room full of eyes looking to you in fear for the answer and the reason. When that happens, will you be ready?

There may come a time when your words or deeds—the very thing you say or avoid saying, the very thing you do or decide not to do—will instruct or heal or ease or repair. You may be the one who gives a student a reason to go onward, a feeling that there is a reason for being—if you notice the moment and know how to respond to it. Those moments approach. Will you be ready?

There may come a time when a student sees in you something that can be trusted, something you may not even see in yourself. That student may ask, "Would you still like me if I were gay?" Or another student may tell you that she was pregnant but now she is bleeding, or about the vile acts of family members, or that Grandpa has to die and can you please help? You will remember that you were taught to teach verb tense and polynomials. But now can you help, should you help, how?

So many people are wary of being a teacher. They prefer pallid synonyms like "facilitator." This is not your fate. You want to teach because you know that more lives have been touched and more lives have been saved in the space between a teacher's desk and a student's desk than in any other: surgeon and patient, pastor and flock. This is no mere *sage on the stage* conceit. You want to be their teacher. You want to be ready.

How Does One Become Ready to Teach?

In the course of my time behind the big desk, I was engaged in the lives of some 3,500 young people. With some I failed miserably;

with most it worked out. What I write about successful teaching may or may not be a template for you, but it will describe my passion, for I believe that only with passion can you succeed as a teacher. But passion alone is not the answer. If it were, then anyone could get up there. All the passion in the world for teaching children will not offer you success if you have little passion for or knowledge of subject content or teaching strategy. All the knowledge in the world about subject content will not help you if you have no passion for people.

The search for a balance between your passions will occupy you throughout your career. Few careers have as much at stake for so many as teaching. Air traffic controllers control hundreds of people by the very things they say and decide. But they do not see or smell them as they decide. The family physician heals by word and deed and makes as many decisions of import. But few of them outside the operating room or the emergency room have to decide instantly about the right thing to do, in a crowd, the clock ticking. Police officers keep harmony and contend with a wide spectrum of life. But few of them have fifteen to thirty citizens together in one room demanding in their earnest way what you've been entrusted to provide.

My students from years ago occasionally return to say, "You remember when you said . . . ?" or "Remember when you wrote . . . ?" and "That really helped, thanks." In fact, I don't even remember what I had for breakfast that morning, but like Velcro the moments I had with them have been held, for good or naught. As teachers we have the power to create so much good or naught that if you think about it too long you freeze up, like trying to command your breathing. But you have to say something up there, don't you? Even when you hear the doubter in your head whisper, "You're faking. They know." Soon, your paranoia reasons, the door will open and the principal or the truth police will pour in, and they will point you to the exit. Why didn't anybody in college tell you it was going to be this real, this raw, this critical?

Starting in 1976, I began to find purpose and meaning in my life by helping children find purpose and meaning in theirs. Through my errors, through my successes, and through the example of masterful teachers, I was able to carve some beliefs about the craft and art of this noble but maligned profession.

Socrates is long dead, yet we still continue his method of imparting information and inspiring learning in a cloistered room with one person leading children in activities. This is called teaching.

Only those in the profession recognize its oddity. Do you remember your speech classes in high school? Standing in front of people, exposing all you are, what you look like, how you talk, how you think in front of a group of bored people not wanting to hear what you have to say? Within seconds after starting, that little voice in your head began to speak to you: *"They're looking at me. They know I have no idea what I'm talking about, and they have no interest. I could spontaneously combust right here in front of them. Oh, why was I born?"*

Do thoughts like that seem too farfetched? Wait until you stand in front of students, hundreds of them all day long. Five classes daily (if you're a high school teacher), 185 days or so per year, fifty minutes per class period: that's 45,000 minutes of class time. That's 15,000 three-minute speeches in one school year! Your students will sit because our culture prefers its students to sit while looking at you. You'll look at your students because our culture prefers its teachers to keep eyes opened when facing students. You'll open your mouth to speak because the primary communication medium our culture uses in the classroom is the spoken word. And within minutes you will have not only that voice inside your head judging you, but all your students as well.

What Is a Teacher? A Parable

Envision an average city street, with curb and streetlight on the corner.

On that street corner, three persons converge. One person stands under the streetlight, merely waiting for something to happen.

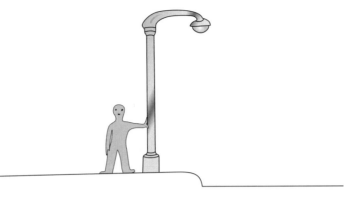

Another person walks by, his head adorned with a hat. Not just any hat, but a *cool* hat, for this person is ultimate cool. People may be starving around him, but he is unconcerned. Hunger and despair abound, no problem. Cool Hat has no worries, need not see. All he does is walk down the street unconcerned, cool hat over his eyes.

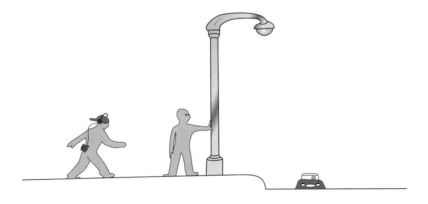

The third person in our story now approaches behind the wheel of a car. Regardless of the circumstances, he approaches, fast.

Set the play in motion. Cool Hat walks down the street. Does he notice the person under the street lamp? Of course not. So cool and so unconcerned is he about all that is around him that he steps off the curb neither knowing nor seeing that Driver soon will turn him into a warm pool of protoplasm on the proverbial street.

But Person Under the Streetlamp sees the impending danger. And because Person sees, Person speaks. It need not be anything eloquent, not anything long, just a simple, "Heyyyy! . . ."

. . . will do. And that's just enough for Cool Hat to stop, look up, note the car's approach, curse, and step out of the way. Away goes Driver, headed wherever. Cool Hat, his cool momentarily ruffled, readjusts his hat and, a bit more warily, continues his journey. And Person Under the Streetlamp remains.

This parable explains the reason for teaching. At various times we are all Cool Hat, blithely believing we can journey on without need of notice or care for anyone, comforted by the soft false assurance our cool hats provide. Lately I've been thinking it may be time to replace the cool hat symbol in this parable with an even more common symbol of modern isolation and unconcern, an iPod.

Nothing inside Cool Hat's head could have saved him from becoming that warm pool of protoplasm on the proverbial street. But it was what was inside the head of Person Under the Streetlamp that entered Cool Hat's head, and that activated Cool Hat, caused his reaction, saved him from harm. The ironic truth about Person Under the Streetlamp is that Person was under no obligation to say anything. But he did.

Person Under the Streetlamp is the teacher, the voice of all, living or dead, from whom we have learned, all the people in our lives who by the words uttered brought us knowledge. Whether classroom teacher, parent, author, songwriter, poet, or playwright, the Person Under the Streetlamp is anyone whose words enter our minds in time to allow us to react, sometimes in time to avoid the full effect of injury from the Driver sitting behind the wheel of the Car of Life.

Our life journeys provide us with many cars hurtling toward us. For high school seniors, the most easily seen is the car called College. Many whom I've taught when they were big fish in the small pond of high school left for the University of Somewhere and the possibility of being flattened by the strength of the challenge that awaited them. For all of us, there will be an unavoidable car called Loss. How we recover and continue after that collision depends upon the quality of the words in our heads under our cool hats. Our teachers' words are the ones that allow us to move onward through our grief.

Teachers are the key to surviving. That's where you come in. You are Person Under the Streetlamp, waiting. You are under no obligation to provide anything for the Cool Hats who saunter past you for a time. But you know the Street and what it contains. And something within you compels you to utter words to the Cool Hats as they pass, and what you say and do may be what remains under their cool hats, allowing them to move forward further down the street, safely.

Remember that responsibility the next time someone outside the profession lambastes you for taking off June, July, and August. Think about your critics standing in your shoes for a week, withering under your responsibility and challenge. You could certainly fare well in their jobs, staring at a computer screen or screaming numbers in a trade room. But after that your heart would ache for those moments in the company of children, where what you do and what you say mean so much.

I Know This Much Is True

Methodologies may change and styles may differ in teaching. But there are some things that transcend the momentary and the regional in teaching. I have Penny Lundquist, my colleague at Golden Apple, to thank for this compilation of items to comment upon. This much, I warrant, is true in all states and territories:

1. *Teachers do not yell at kids.* Reread the preceding statement. Read it again. The minute you raise your voice you are losing. What can you do instead?

2. *Teachers do not send kids out of the room as a discipline procedure.* Barring threat to health and safety, these are your students, your individual and collective challenge to assess, diagnose, and determine best course of action.

3. *Teachers get and send feedback to students every week.* This
is the central importance of assessment. You receive input to
inform your teaching. Am I going too fast or slow? You provide input to inform your students to inform their learning.
The net effect of this is not only to demonstrate the importance of assessment, but it also indicates to them that their
presence and participation is important to you.

4. *Teachers greet students, welcome them to class and individualize their comments.* Whether it be hearty or casual, eye
contact based or specific words, let your students know their
presence matters to you.

5. *Student work is proudly displayed and student interests are
reflected in the room.* Help make it their room (that is, if you
have the opportunity to claim a wall or two, unless you are
an itinerant teacher traveling amongst multiple rooms, which
makes this truth challenging but not impossible).

6. *Students manage classroom tasks and have roles and
responsibilities.* These may vary and may be spread out
amongst the school year, but giving your class time structure
and dimension cues them to your impression that they too
have an important role to play in their learning.

7. *Teachers never embarrass children, never use sarcasm nor
ostracize, nor publicly or privately humiliate a child.* While
you repeat #1 frequently, I wish all teachers would tattoo this
truth on their psyches, if not their bodies.

8. *Teachers give equal opportunities to female and male
students on the left side and right side of the classroom to
answer questions, receive praise, and assume responsibilities.* New teachers are surprisingly narrow in their classroom
visual acuity and often clueless in their leaning toward one
gender and even one side of the classroom. If possible, have
a colleague observe you with a classroom skein on them
marking which students are called upon to respond or make
comments.

9. *A teacher makes every student believe he or she is the
teacher's favorite.* This may be more hope than truth, and
the hardest of these truths to activate, but try it anyway.

10. *Instructional time is not wasted.* So much precious instruction time is winnowed away by test preparation, announcements over the airwaves, and unavoidable circumstances. Try not to add to this by filling time with work sheet completion, time off task, last five or ten or fifteen minutes of free time for desultory gossiping or pretend focus on homework. Teach bell to bell as if you don't have enough time to teach them all you want them to learn. For you know what? You don't.

11. *Teachers let absent children know they are missed.* I used to call my students when absent. At first it freaked them out. Parents loved it, but students got the message: this doesn't work as well as it can without you. I know when you're not around and I rue it, whether legitimate illness or feigned excuse. Letting them know you know lets them know it matters.

12. *Teachers post in their classroom a statement of their commitment to their students.* I long to see a world where in each classroom words of importance are displayed. "Who you are, what you say, your being here matters a great deal." Or "I will always treat you fairly and with respect." Even better—compose in coordination with your students what this statement will be. It becomes the contractual arrangement classrooms truly are. More on that in the next chapter.

REFLECTIVE EXERCISE

Complete one statement about what will always be true in your classroom. Try this:

Regardless of what occurs in my life or in my school, in my classroom there will always be

_____

Save this statement.

CHAPTER SEVEN

The Teacher's Words

You Can Heal and You Can Harm

W ords are the inescapable vehicle by which the teacher imparts, inspires, questions, appraises, and reflects to students. All teachers would be wise to acquire a healthy command of and respect for words. I heard about research done in the 1960s that determined that the average seventeen-year-old has a working command of 15,000 to 20,000 words. Now how they performed this study has always mystified me. Did they take an average seventeen-year-old, sit him or her in a room with paper and pen, and command, "Write every word you know!" How would such a teen respond? The cynic in me envisions the list: *"a, and, the, dude, party . . ."* and so on. Over one million words in the English language, and regardless of our years of experience or education, each of us commands just a fraction of those words. But the things done with them!

WORD ALCHEMY

Example: Ordinarily, masses of students pass each other in school hallways each day. Some mutter *hi* or *hello* or *yo* causing nary a pause save a smile or a nod. But if *that* person you know, the answer to one's prayers, the person who could make life complete walks past with an, "I like your hair today," . . . well, observe the reaction. The heart races, the sweat glands open, the tongue thickens, and the student *garumphs* a response, all which is code for *I am noticed!*

That person is here! Let us rejoice! The words echo throughout the school day and then sing out through the evening through telephone cables and across cyberspace. *I am noticed! That person is here! Let us rejoice!* All for words.

Every word has its history—fascinating in its development and use. Consider the anarchists who needed to ingest hashish before carrying out murderous attacks against political leaders. They became known as the "hashish eaters," in Arabic *hashshashin,* creating our present-day word "assassin." Of somewhat lesser import, consider the Middle Dutch phrase *wijssegger,* or wise speaker, origin of the American "wiseacre." The history of words can fascinate.

Our minds contain the histories of the words we know and use. Experiment—watch how easy this is to enact. Ready? *Bear.* Ping into your mind comes the image. I'll refine and specify: *white bear.* Ping there it is. Now stop thinking about white bear—no more white bear. Yet for awhile you'll wander to other paragraphs thinking and seeing *white bear . . . white bear. . . .*

Now think *yellow.* Your mind dutifully provides history: a color, a pejorative term implying cowardice. Perhaps some symbols appear, for example, the sun or a songbird. Now take another word, one with its own separate history and place it alongside: *yellow . . . snow.* Ping ping you now see a third image appear, an image that wasn't in *yellow* or in *snow,* but in their juxtaposition. Yellow snow—that which you should not. . . . Yes!

I call this the Frank Zappa Memorial Yellow Snow Word Usage Theory, after his song using the same title (1974).Word juxtaposition creates images that were not there in the words by themselves. Not only can these positions create images, they can evoke physical reaction as well. Consider: *bloody pus*—your mind images and makes you think, "Yuck!" Or *uneven teeth*—your mind images and tempts you to judge a person so described. So powerful are words that their placement can create image and convey mood.

Now think about the images created and the moods conveyed in class by the words "Darlene, that was a stupid thing to say." Or the words "Shut up!" which certainly convey more to students listening more than the order to become quiet.

Think of the unkind things teachers have said to you over the course of your schooling. You may not remember much about the subjects they taught, but if a teacher said something hurtful to you fifteen years ago, you remember it chapter and verse. Sadly, the unkind things said to students often return as self-fulfilled prophecy. Told you're dumb, you'll think so. Told women can't achieve in math, it'll happen. But consider this: Tell students that they have a purpose in life, and they'll acquire one. Tell them that they can, and they will. Show them that they can, and they will surpass. The very words you use as a teacher can heal and cause success to happen. The very words you use as a teacher can cause harm and limit potential. The very words you use.

During my early teaching years, I taught summer school classes for juniors who had failed English 11. Given the freedom to do what I wanted, I presented the curriculum I had used for the Honors English 11 class. The summer school students read the poems, wrote the papers, succeeded. At the end of the summer term, I told them they had achieved with honors material. "But we're dumb," one confessed, almost as a shield as well as a wound. "Someone told you that," I replied, "and lied."

The power of words is in your hands as a teacher. With words, you can heal and you can harm. The children in your classrooms are well versed in the use of words as missiles, fully aware of the harm they cause in shouting *fag, bimbo, dumb blonde, geek, drama queen.* You should strive to make your classrooms a zone free from harmful words.

Words. Respect them and use them with knowledge of what they can do.

WORDS AS CONTRACT IN
SOCIETY AND IN THE CLASSROOM

Words also denote a contractual arrangement. As a student, you most likely spent many cold mornings or afternoons waiting for a school bus to pick you up. The bus driver did indeed pick you up, even though no power forced him or her to do so. The bus driver could have entered the vehicle thinking, "Today, I will go to the dunes!" and could have driven past the cold and shivering students shouting, "Today, the dunes!" But the driver stopped, greeted, transported. Why? Words.

You say to a student, "See me after your last class." That student's future is now altered. No longer can she travel with friends over to the mall after school because you altered her future. If the student arrives and you aren't there, she will look at you funny the next day as you apologize and say, "Really, come by afterward today." Be not there again, and you are deemed untrustworthy. Your contract is not good. Why? Words.

You walk among your students. They sit in rows perfectly confident that you are not going to take a swing at any of them, even though you have the power to do so, even though you may harbor the desire to do so. But they sit perfectly comfortable in the unspoken agreement. You will not harm them, even though you could. Why? Words.

The bus driver signed a contract with implied words that on specific days at specific locations, all those who look like they're heading for school will be picked up and transported. You signed a contract with society, whether actual or implied, that allows you access to children in the promise that you will not harm them. So you do not. Your word is your contract.

We exist as a society by means of an amazing irony. We live in freedom by voluntarily giving up our freedom. We have the freedom to hit, but we do not. We have the freedom to drive to the dunes on a workday, but we do not. We have the freedom to drive through red lights, but we do not.

The very notion of civil disobedience is predicated on people activating the freedoms they have but normally suppress. Your students do not move en masse out the door of your classroom before the bell rings, even though they have the freedom to do so and probably at times harbor the desire. What prevents them all from leaving? Nothing.

If they were particularly incensed at some injustice that occurred at school, they could walk out in protest, march to the nearest intersection, and sit down in the street, arms locked. If they were to act on their freedom to do just that, the cars approaching them would have the freedom to run them over but would not act on that freedom even if gridlock ensued. If gridlock were to ensue, police would be called in to clear the intersection, arresting those who refuse to move while news helicopters hover overhead. Then the arrested would have to be processed, overburdening the local police station or courthouse. The entire free flow of society might grind to a halt to accommodate those who act on the freedom they ordinarily relinquish in order to be a part of society.

Similarly, the society of your classroom depends upon a voluntary relinquishing of freedom. It is up to you to help foster meaning and peace and safety and dimension within your classroom. That is your contract. We have the freedom to choose chaos, but we crave order. We have the freedom to lie, but we strive for truth.

WORDS AS MAPS TO THE
TERRITORY OF YOUR CLASSROOM

Our words create maps of the territory others experience. In *Language in Thought and Action* (1949/1991), a semantics text seminal in the development of my teaching, S. I. Hayakawa discussed the map-territory distinction. It is a strong basis upon which to understand the power of words as they relate to your position as a teacher.

To simplify Hayakawa's semantic perception: *maps* are words that attempt to define the *territory* of reality. Maps are not the territory itself; rather they are approximations of the territory, since our perceptions of reality differ and our words do not exactly reflect the reality of life.

We grow up and learn life by means of a series of maps presented to us of how the world works. The maps come from those closest to us, those we encounter, what we read, what we experience. Trouble is many of our maps are false representations of reality, and we go through life trying to rework the false maps we are given. This is the key reason prejudice exists, a matter I'll reserve for closer discussion in Chapter 9.

Like many of you, I have participated in the deliberate creation of false maps, sometimes knowingly and lovingly. When my wife and I gave our daughter the false map known as Santa Claus, it was with a desire to extend to her a belief in the love and generosity of the world. Then came that damn day when she brought home the words from her fellow third graders. "Mom, Dad," she sniffed at the dinner table, "the kids at school told me there's no Santa Claus. Isn't there?"

My wife and I looked at each other with the "here we go" knowing look that our false map made inevitable. I tried to use my wordsmith powers to extend her childhood a little more: "Well, Mary Beth, if you took all the love in the world and gave it a human face, Santa's would be that face." Not bad, right? Of course, she saw through it instantly.

"But Dad, is there?"

Another look from my wife indicated that now I was on my own, so there I went into that dark place where map and territory collide. "No dear, there really isn't."

"Boohoo!" wailed my daughter, bolting from the table and running upstairs to bed. "Boohoo!" sobbed my wife, running after her to spend the night with our daughter's tears. And Dad remained alone with the unfinished meal pondering the sad world of map-territory displacement.

The next morning, my swollen-eyed daughter and I hid from each other behind cereal boxes. Her attack was simple, yet relentless. "Dad, the Easter Bunny?"

I wished for a larger box of cereal. "Uh, no, honey."

"The tooth fairy?"

Sigh and double sigh: "No, baby, no tooth fairy either."

Then she became indignant: "God?"

"Well yes, baby, in our house, there is God."

In measures small and large, what you do in the classroom creates maps for your students representing your perception of the territory you are teaching. Hayakawa believed that words impart two things: a body of knowledge and a way of holding that body of knowledge.

The words that you use create not just maps for your students. They also represent a contractual arrangement. Even though no power compels them, your students for the most part will remain in your classroom and will pay attention to you unless and until you give them a reason to abandon caring about you. And you will remain with them, voluntarily giving up your freedom to be elsewhere, presenting to them through words both a body of knowledge and a way of holding the body of knowledge you wish them to discover.

Your every word and action, as well as your every silence and inaction, will communicate meaning to your students. I hope your words match reality as accurately as a map describes a territory. When given the choice, I hope you choose words that heal, clarify, support, and inspire. I hope your words are contractually sound. But before they can be, you must know your reasons for standing by the big desk at the front of the classroom.

The Value of Praise

Praise is the necessary unguent of movement and advancement of your teaching goals. Used without art and recklessly, praise becomes inutile. Used with precision and sincerity, it gives students the intimation of a growing sense of their confidence and improvement.

Praise can be directed toward the students' minds (they do, say, write something particularly well) or toward their hearts (congratulatory exhalations of their accomplishments). Sincerity moves. Practice praise with care and watch them risk more, listen with intent, risk more frequently. Grow. All from your words. Such power you can wield to heal or harm.

REFLECTIVE EXERCISE

List the words you know never to use in front of students. I know you won't curse in front of them, so think deeper to the words you know could hurt or limit them. Make a small sign with those words in a crossed circle. Paste them in your grade book. Give $100 to your favorite charity every time you falter.

CHAPTER EIGHT

The Teaching Persona

Who You Are When You're Standing Up There at the Big Desk

In Robert Penn Warren's (1996) novel *All the King's Men,* the main character Jack Burden muses as he drives in the rain about all the versions of himself he has portrayed in his life. The person he was in school was not the person he was in the story's present, running political cover for his Louisiana governor. The person he was with his former wife was not the person he was with his childhood sweetheart and forever lover. The person he was in the car at that time driving alone in the rain resembled none of the other manifestations of himself. Who was the real one? This sort of musing is Basic Irony 101. Who are you really? In *Language in Thought and Action* (1949/1991), S. I. Hayakawa recognizes the differences in what we project to others as our understanding of different semantic environments. We present ourselves to different people differently. We do not speak to our pastor as we do to our spouse. We do not use street slang in the work place. We do not speak to our parents as we do our friends. We know how to adjust our language to fit the environments in which we find ourselves. And we know how to adjust our *selves* to fit our environments. We change ourselves as easily as we change our shirts. Are these other selves false images? Or are they rather facets of the person we are, revealed by specific circumstances? When we adjust and when we alter, we are not donning false maps any more than we are different when we change clothes. We respond to circumstances and show a facet of ourselves appropriate to a specific environment.

How You Present Yourself
in Your Classroom

This discussion leads us to consider how you will present yourself in your classroom. Many novice teachers believe they must ruthlessly omit all aspects of their personality to present Teacher Animatron who does not smile until some holiday passes. Others believe only an absolutely faithful presentation of one's true self is honest enough. Both impressions have their faults.

To show little of yourself to your students clouds your effectiveness. But if you present yourself "warts and all" to your students, you will also, ironically, lose effectiveness. Your personal life will sometimes weigh heavily upon your ability to work. As department chair, I once walked past a colleague's classroom and observed her weeping in front of her ninth-grade students. Under certain circumstances, showing emotion is appropriate, but my instincts led me to enter the room that day and ask if she wished me to sit with her students while she left the room to compose herself. Later, she divulged that she had been detailing part of her marital discord and impending divorce to her students when her emotions got the better of her. My response was part sharp, part compassionate: What did she hope to gain by presenting her emotional pain to fourteen- and fifteen-year-olds, some of whom were doubtless dealing with their own painful emotions? What did she hope to receive from them? Advice? Sympathy? Were they equipped to offer either? Should they be expected to provide either?

What students look for in their teachers is a combination of sensitivity and strength. We adults all deal with the challenges of life: our aging, the aging of those we love, love's inconstancy, disappointment, betrayal, isolation, separation, and death. Should we project our struggle with all these challenges to the children we teach? Will that prepare them for the disappointments they will face as adults?

The persona we project to our students as teachers is an amalgam of who we are. The classroom is a semantic environment where we mix hope and struggle. Your students need to see you as someone who has reached a point of triumph over travail, both academic and personal, while continuing to cope with the pressures of life. Your presence in front of them serves as a role model of potential they can look to for hope for their own struggles. This does not mean that you do not show concern or doubt. But neither should you reflect hopelessness or futility, even if you are besieged by such demons. If you let them, your students will feed off your negativity as surely as they will acquire nurture from your energy and your strength.

There is a further, practical advantage to your developing a teaching persona. It can provide an appropriate boundary for those times when students clamor for more information about you, perhaps to extend sympathy or to delay an assignment. "Tell us about the sixties," was, for teachers of my generation, an invitation to slip into the nostalgic haze of youth. But are there not some questions that you might not want to answer: "Did you take drugs then?" "Do you now?" "Did you live with a lover?" "Do you now?" "Did the FBI collect information about you?" "Were you ever arrested?" Such questions, even if innocently asked, can paint the teacher into a corner if the teacher is overly concerned about detailing a "true" self.

So how do you go about constructing your teaching persona? Is it like studying acting or speech?

HOW YOU ASK QUESTIONS

Key elements in the development of your teaching persona are

- The way you ask questions
- The kinds of questions you ask
- The philosophic stance you evince to your students as you ask questions

I believe asking questions is an art form, one that requires diligent practice and skill.

As a novice teacher, you may start out much the way I did, with a prepared list of questions. I recall with sad nostalgia my first year as a teacher, when I asked my prepared questions and received answers, or silence, or what I thought were erroneous answers. I read through my list of questions, looked up at their end, and noted with nervousness that much time remained and I had no idea where to go. Perhaps the following suggestions will save you some of those awkward moments.

Don't advertise that you know the answer to every question you ask. Even if you have studied the topic of the day until you feel as if you coined the idea yourself, try not to show an "I know it, you don't, and I will ask questions until your thoughts match mine" mode. That stance reduces question-asking to a tiresome game that does not promote thought. I aimed to approach a subject with an earnest befuddlement—not so extreme as to suggest I was a dolt on the subject, but abundantly clear that in the investigation of a topic, we were discovering answers together. This tack will be difficult if you have the kind of personality that must always know and project that superiority. If that is your personality, then you have already projected it in your classroom. Your students will be loathe to consider questions if you already know the answer.

Use the answer of one student to prompt the next question. "Tom, what Janet says about this topic has some merit. Does it match what you feel about this subject?" Rather than lean on a prepared list of questions, weave new questions out of the fabric of your students' answers.

Don't be afraid of silence. Novice teachers often get skittish about silence and proceed to answer all their own questions, thereby cueing students on how the class will work—just allow the teacher to ask and answer without interference or participation. If you find yourself confronting silence, I would recommend looking at the kind of questions you are asking. Do they require mere repetition of material, or do they ask the students to move to deeper levels? Do you see the difference between the question, "Where are the letters to Celie hidden in *The Color Purple?*" and the question, "Is it wrong under every circumstance to keep letters from someone? What if your parent wanted to hide something from you? Is that always wrong?"

Do not ask questions that make students defensive. "What did you think of the book?" you ask.

"I hated it," someone responds.

"Why did you hate it?"

"Because I did, that's why" is the likely and appropriate response.

Such questions make students defend themselves for fear of being made to look fools. Avoid such questions. Liking or not liking something is not the highest level of discussion to consider. Finding the relevant connection to the students' lives is the more appropriate goal.

Avoid questions that begin with "What about . . . ?" These are questions with circular answers. The appropriate retort will be "Well, what about it?"

Avoid false praise. Praise responses that strike you as sound, but do not praise every sentence your students utter. Students are remarkably adept at detecting false praise. They will pick up on insincere and indiscriminate praise as readily as they will someone who absolutely cannot offer positive comment to anyone. In either extreme lies disregard and disrespect for students. Conversely:

Use praise adroitly. Judicious use of superlatives reaches students' minds and hearts simultaneously. When they know you are sincere in praising them, followed by a reason for such high praise, you have brought tenacity and resilience to students' thinking. Your belief in them solves so much!

Be aware of how you choose respondents. My colleagues were always amazed when I noted that they asked more questions of males than of females or that they called on students predominantly on one side of the room over the other. Become aware of your patterns.

Always let them talk! Do not be a slave to the tyranny of coverage, of time constraints, of what's next on your lesson plan. When the hands go up, let them talk. Weave their answers to the next point, praise, and avoid the pontification gene in you that wishes to get them to where you want them to be by telling them what you think. The point is to let them get there, not by your force, but by their discussion. So get out of their way. The absolute best part of classroom discussion is when they take it over, leaving you to be the adroit and focused air traffic controller who directs speaking order. Don't say, "Okay, this is the last comment we'll take on this subject—we have to keep moving." Stay on their schedule, not yours, unless, of course, you note that there are precious few seconds left in the class period.

Become a student of the art of asking questions as a way of opening your students to discussion and to critical thinking.

How You Decorate Your Classroom

Your teaching persona is also revealed in the educational atmosphere you foster. The way in which you organize and adorn your room, if you are fortunate to have your own classroom, offers many messages to children.

Many new teachers are itinerant travelers, bravely chugging along the halls with their stuff in tow on a cart of some kind. It's an awful way to treat professionals and if it happens to you, I hope you get a room of your own next year, even if you have to share with another teacher. When you have actual wall space, then you have the real opportunity to make your room reflect your teaching tenets (more about tenets in Chapter 3). In this manner, elementary teachers have an understanding stronger than their secondary colleagues, many of whom never bother with anything but the simplest of wall decor, such as fire drill instructions or a sports team poster.

Your classrooms should be as well thought out as your lesson plans. Classroom decor will give your students something to stare at while feigning interest in what you're doing and still allow them to be engaged in something associated with the philosophy you have devised. The best teachers work in the most fascinating environments, rich in stimuli and complicated in design, some with and some without riches in technology or resources. The classrooms that demonstrate care and creativity have a design and a purpose. Such teachers know how children perceive and engage.

You can look around your own school for the creative and intriguing teachers. Ask the children—they'll tell you instantly who has captivated them. Then look at the surroundings of that teacher's room and watch her work. Note the persona she projects and ask her later what animates and inspires her teaching. You will always receive a well-articulated sense of mission animating a clearly reflected persona. The excellent teacher does not free-form a lesson like an improvised jazz riff. The great teacher does not work off the cuff. He or she proceeds as a result of inspired reflection and dogged practice.

"TELL ME WHAT YOU THINK OF ME"

Recognizing and Understanding
Your Teaching Persona

In a darkened room, thirty prospective teachers sit in a half circle. In the center of the room, lit by a lone light, a single chair is placed. A volunteer stands, walks to the chair, and faces the room. After stating his or her name, the volunteer asks, "Tell me what you think of me," and sits in the chair.

Once seated, the volunteer cannot speak. Those who are gathered around are instructed that they are free to respond or not to respond to the question. If responding, they must do so in complete sentences. After a prescribed interval, a moderator calls, "Time." The seated one then rises, saying only, "Thank you." The next one volunteers and the process is repeated.

This activity has been the culminating exercise in my work with prospective teachers for over two decades. I refer to it as the LaSalle exercise because I first experienced it at a religious retreat at LaSalle Manor in Plano, Illinois. I use it now not for religious revelation but to guide prospective teachers. They have studied the teaching profession as an art form. They have witnessed teaching styles that range from awesome to awful through their school site observations. They have brought their preconceived notions about what it means to teach and their preconceived notions about race and gender and children. Through the conversations and arguments and reflection, they are brought to a chair to ask others what they think of them.

This exercise reverses the presumed power polarity in a classroom. The person up front, supposedly singular and powerful, wields no power and cannot speak once seated in the chair. The gathered, usually perceived as submissive to the will of the teacher, hold in their hands the self-esteem of the one seated.

Can you imagine any of your teachers in such a chair, in such a position? The tension is palpable, yet those in the room are drawn to volunteer. These prospective teachers want so much to be up there, by the big desk, in charge. This moment challenges that desire.

What occurs around that chair can be breathtaking, life changing, and hard to describe unless witnessed. The gathered tell the one seated, in honest and humble tones, what they have seen. The gathered hold their power as it should always be held, gingerly and respectfully. Hope abounds. Honest advice is given. Colleagues form bonds that continue throughout their teaching careers. Copious tears are shed as is appropriate whenever professionals engage in a risky activity and are rewarded with useful information for the next stage of their development as teachers.

REFLECTIVE EXERCISES

1. Look back on the journey of your life. Can you hear the voices of your past? Can you hear the voices that shaped you, taught you, that gave you the tools to pursue the purpose and meaning for which you now search?

2. Now stretch your mind forward. Can you hear the voices of your future students? Can you hear their laughter, their questions, their anger, their joy, their thanks?

3. Next time you find yourself in conversation, try to step back and observe yourself. Do you appear natural and animated or stiff and formal? Do you dominate conversation or add to it?

4. Ask your friends about the way you project yourself in conversation. That is your first step to developing your own teacher persona.

Will you be ready?

CHAPTER NINE

Working With Colleagues

Being a Team Player

Positioning yourself to be perceived as a team player is a valuable exercise in determining whether you have found a school to remain and grow in and colleagues who can help you mature in your work and feel kinship. Like any job setting, the school is populated with a wide range of people: joyous and lifeless, trustworthy and devious, cynical and callous, hopeful and buoyant. While observing the scene and discovering who is whom, the natural tendency is to be shy, withdrawn, not yourself. I suggest the opposite tactic. Start out being who you are and give off a sense of openness and congeniality. That way, the waves you send out bounce off the people you meet who flash vestiges of their true selves immediately. More than most job settings, schoolteacher talk gravitates toward a perceived power order. Whoever believes you pose a threat to their perception of status will show their quills. Whoever cares not a jot about such hooey will return serve with equal warmth. The ones whose ambitious striving on the way up reveal themselves as clearly as the ones who are awash in their misery. Gestures, eye movements, vocal tone—we exude visual fingerprints of our personality content. You'll know who to sit next to and confide in and those from whom you'll remain wary and polite.

Sometimes the circumstances of your employment find you sharing classrooms with another teacher, and the rules of dorm life come into play. You'll see who'll cede space from those who zealously guard every piece of floor tile as if it was dedicated to them by the goddess of teachers. My goodness, such anxiety emanates from the hoarder and protector! In a business where power is truly ephemeral, some in our profession just manufacture it out of the purest of nothingness. "I've been here longer, so I deserve all the desk drawers!" How sad. You get a paycheck too; you're on the faculty list in alpha order with the robber baron, so stand your ground with the nicest of smiles.

The coin of realm in teaching is stuff. You'll have little, and they have lots. You'd think sharing in such an egalitarian setting would be commonplace—but be prepared for someone who figures they earned their materials, test questions and lesson plan approaches, and you can just wither away without their assistance. Some teachers are great and open about sharing, and they will help you compose the teacher persona you'll so quickly note you lack. Of course, it is a mistake to think that possession of the stuff (yours or others) will help you become the teacher you need to be. That path lies within you and the preparation and reflection you have made to meet these first days. Teaching is not teacher-proof—you cannot just open someone else's notes or pass out someone else's assignments and think that anything more than time will pass.

The one true thing your colleagues who have been there longer have over you is knowledge of the place and a stronger sense of confidence about their teacher persona. The better ones know why they are there, and their stuff serves to animate and illustrate that purpose. You are fumbling because you sense you are just rocketing from lecture to assignment to discussion without a clue as to why besides the guilt coverage provides you. Hanging around teachers you trust will help you learn and unburden and receive tips. Those who are kind enough to allow true induction to take place will help you open yourself to the path of knowing why you teach. The administration will provide their array of induction must-go-to-meetings that wander about the periphery of what it means to be a dutiful employee. The real heart of discovery about teaching will not occur there. You'll be so afraid of exhibiting doubt and difficulty you won't recognize the *you* who attends those meetings. Administrators expect you to know why you're spending time there. The truly gifted ones will approach you with the wisdom and sensitivity of a guild master to an apprentice and exhibit insight about your misperceptions and fears. But the ones you work next to and along with could be persons you can trust—as long as, and note carefully this codicil—*you do not seek or initiate such consult? in the teacher's lounge.* Find the teacher who believes true collegial discussion about reaching higher levels of teaching accomplishment takes place in the teacher's lounge, and you will have either a liar or a cynic in disguise. Think of the other jobs you may have had—and consider the workroom or the lunchroom or the break room therein. What went on in those rooms? Ribald humor? Relentless, anarchistic diatribes against the powerful, obtuse, clueless, or dopey? Mean-spirited double entendre? Outright mimicry and mockery—not only of colleagues but of superiors as well? What makes you think the teacher's lounge is free of those elements? People go to the lounge to decompress their depression, focus on what they cannot compartmentalize, eat lunch in deeply desired and transient peace. The advice and council you seek will not be happening there.

Some circumstances provide you with a second teacher or aide in the room. With inclusion, you may have a colleague in your class helping one student or a group of students identified with individual learning plans. This sharing of space and help has its good and challenging sides. When the aide is of quality, the effects can be quite strong as you work in tandem to differentiate instruction and offer special attention where needed. When the assistance is less than ideal it can be quite burdensome. Cross purposes and mind games of who controls this space or lesson may sap your already exhausted resolve. Here yet is another facet of the practice needing discussion in teacher preparation pathways. When the aide is less than adequate, you allow him or her to do the job without letting it impact your primary responsibility for the entire classroom. Some aides, sensing your youth and inexperience, will play power games seeing if they can take advantage of your nice-person demeanor and inexperience. Give them as much niceness as is digestible but clearly articulate it is your professional prognoses that dominates and decides.

In Martin Haberman's (1995) *Star Teachers of Children in Poverty,* much credit is given to the teacher who establishes a core support system within the school. He depicts this activity as a healthy deterrent to burn out. The teacher who goes it alone, who feels the best way to relieve the stresses of the profession is to take courses or vacations ignores the necessary value of like-minded educators banding together for personal succor and student success.

In short, your time as a faculty member will be filled with challenge and opportunity. Most times you are among kindred and dedicated professionals. You'll sense who to avoid and who gets your "steel magnolia" treatment of polite and firm resolve. You have a license to be with and work with children. Earn it by keeping a welcome eye open for those who can deepen your knowledge and a resolve to block those who will attempt to sap your confidence or fill you with bile. You enter a teaching community, and like all communities, it has its elements that allow you to depict the community as beneficial and nurturing, superficial and docile, or enervating and deleterious. The savvy you earn over your years of interaction should not fail you even though you feel like a new person. Watch, weigh, and consider the actions and words of your colleagues, and from that base you will know how to proceed.

REFLECTIVE EXERCISE

Task: Take five colleagues, study them, write in your journal your impressions of them and how you derived those impressions. Revisit those thoughts three or four times over the course of the school year. Have those thoughts strengthened or altered?

CHAPTER TEN

Dealing With School Hierarchy and Politics

You get your first assignment, and your focus is on the necessary and mundane. You practice the drive to the school to check traffic conditions so you never arrive late. You purchase sufficient materials to make your room attractive and inviting. Once in the building, you memorize routes and routines so you can fit in as seamlessly as possible. You stare inside your classroom at the space and imagine your career unfolding. These are all necessary parts of the acclimation phase of your first couple years, but there is one element frequently overlooked that could adversely affect that initial time. New teachers must realize that their impact on the school goes beyond what occurs within their classrooms. New teachers enter a school, a place that is a learning environment, of course, but is also a political environment, one in which the rules of engagement are subtly drawn and visible to the perceptive and reflective, and those who do not exert effort understanding the machinations of a school will ultimately be drawn into its adverse elements.

Your first thought is that the political study of a school is anathema to your reason for entering it. It's supposed to be all about the children, and if everyone within the school are also all about the children, then that force will dominate policy and procedure and those enforcing policy and establishing procedure will certainly act as if of one mind, a community that interacts with altruism and civility. It does not take too long for the perceptive person to note that the school, like every work place, operates under the mission, but those inside interpret it in such sundry ways there'll be days when you wonder how the doors get open at all. Remember in school environments power is truly in the hands of the few, so many within the building manufacture power out of sheer air and bravura, on the basis of proximity or tenure. Who holds the keys, not the metaphoric ones, I mean the actual keys, presumes authority. So in trying to go about in your gosh-I'm-glad-to-be-here first-year teacher way, you may unwittingly find yourself within the cross hairs of those whose seeming existence is focused on the maintenance or demonstration of the pseudo-authority they have created.

How can you detect such actions? Use your powers of observing your students to determine how best to meet their needs and train those powers on the adults with whom you interact throughout the course of the day. Administrative assistants, custodial staff, coaches, librarians, receptionists, assistant principals—each of the office holders within a school has arrived at their positions with some exercise of political acumen. The sensitive should note its elements. Who has the thin skin, who curries favor with the principal, who gabs about the new teachers or students— sometimes right to their face? Which person likes to flaunt their responsibility by cowering others? Who has control over a space—and woe betide those who attempt to use, occupy, store or conduct class within that space without proper obsequies! Where does the prevailing atmosphere of the school come from? If you sense tension or anger in someone at having to work with young people, distrust working with colleagues, detect the dynamics of junior-high level jealousies and manipulations among the adults—observe its sources. Your natural tendency is to seek out those you can count on, unburden with, seek advice from, and receive succor for the stresses and challenges you will encounter. Use those same instincts to understand the political atmosphere you have entered and how you can continue on within that environment without getting sucked into its vortex or worse, be singled out by these sinister elements as the someone-who-does-not-fit-in here, which brings the attention of this dark side to expose your every error and flaw.

Scary, huh? I do not intend to stoke your paranoia. But a healthy amount of political acumen increases your chance for success by understanding the environment you have entered. Of course you see yourself as a change agent, someone who will bring gales of fresh air to the staid school atmosphere you have entered. You are the champion of children, politics be damned, and you will charge ahead and open the musty windows of the-way-it-has-always-been-done to the way things should be! Yes, bless your souls, you may enter with that kind of gusto. Funny thing about school buildings though—they are remarkably like bureaucracies in government, filled with people whose chief talent is to remain, while boss after boss blusters in, predicting mass change, undergo challenge, move on to the next place, to be replaced by, as Pete Townsend would warn you, "Meet the new boss; it's the same as the old boss." School buildings are impressively resistant and imaginatively constructed to confound, exhaust, and disappoint those who do not perceive the prevailing political climate. Change in schools truly comes from within, from those who recognize what exists, resist the temptation to join in, or are victimized by the power games and the gossip chain but who recognize from observation how best to proceed.

How does one proceed? Elements of strength that repel political forces are resiliency, a deep sense of organization, the talent to recognize how one can offend and not be offensive, and yet retain one's sense of what's important. The blusterer who wants to fight every battle and right every wrong perceived in a school building is doomed, just as ironically will the Pollyanna who wishes to ignore whatever political prevalence exists in a school as mere static. The morale in the building must be noticed, and you must decide what your contribution will be to it.

Let's say you note a decidedly antipathetic attitude in your building for students. How could that be, you ask? I know. I once listened to a librarian tell me angrily that if students would not take out the books, the library would be more effective. Uh, really? I also heard a colleague say the favorite part of the school year was final exam week, when most of the students were not in the building. Say what? It exists. So how do you work to counter a prevailing sentiment such as that? You champion your kids in your classroom, yes, and also those in the hall as well. You become known as the person who likes the fact that schools are filled with students, and trust me, students detect that and gravitate to it in gratitude. Now in the prevailing world of the cranky colleagues, where adults sit behind desks hoping students won't come in and will treat them in a desultory way if they do; your presence in their space threatens them. You may have even recognized who the grumpy are. Thing is—you should behave in the same championing manner with adults as you do with students. In Shakespeare's *Othello* (1998), all of Iago's evil manipulative instincts melted when he was in the presence of the goodness of Desdemona. He could not help being evil, and karma came his way thereby, but he was disarmed by the consistency and innate goodness of the person he was trying to undermine to his liege. That is the nature that will serve you well, a sense of transcendent goodness that disarms. That mien will act like an antibiotic, a consistently positive sense of being a part of the community, student and adult alike. It also helps to know which of the administrative assistants, custodial staff, security force, and administration to curry favor with yourself—not to gain power, nor to demean a colleague, but to further a sense that you are a positive part of that community. *That* is how you affect change, by first perceiving well enough to know the environment you have entered and acclimating to its eccentricities and peculiarities of the adults entrusted within it before proceeding more assuredly to positively altering that atmosphere.

This is not the foolproof plan, and you will err, anger someone in the presumed power chain, or step on a toe unwittingly. You learn about what goes on in the classrooms outside your classroom as you do within the classroom assigned you. You may teach, but you are a perpetual, virtual student, learning about technique and motivation inside the classroom, political nuance and power flow outside the classroom. You do not have to become a political animal, but you cannot be naive about political structure within your building. Lest you become perceived as the person who does not "play well in the sandbox" you must develop an awareness of the functioning elements of the community inside your school.

CHAPTER ELEVEN

Don't Make Things Worse

Avoiding Deficit Views of Children

O f course, you will enter your first teaching assignment over-
sensitive to making mistakes—carrying so many governors
on your demeanor that the real you, the one who interacts well with
children, may take a long while to surface. As guarded as you'll be
against offending, you still may unwittingly contribute to the challenges facing you, and that is through the perception you hold of
your students, especially if they are primarily from low-income and
minority backgrounds.

We are uncommonly sensitive to proclaiming we have biases, as
I have discussed in Chapter 7. The insidious nature of bias is based
in our unawareness that we hold them. Bias can be found in the subtextual and the perceptual. How we regard who we teach influences
how we teach. Studies of effective teachers of minority students
(Ladson-Billings, 1994) hint that a precursor to school success is the
extent of a teacher's cultural sensitivity, defined as "the ability to
understand the history, values, perceptions, and behaviors of a particular group of people, without judging these to be better or worse
than those of any other group" (Lazar, Pinto, & Warren, 2006). As
teachers, our instinct to judge is innate. We grade efforts, diagnose
attitude and behavior through non-textual cues, strive for our
students to achieve at a certain level of accomplishment we deem
reachable—all when done carefully are valid extensions of our ability to infer. Yet when we examine our students and their frames of

reference in the light of our own cultural frames, we can hold our students back or delay our understanding at how best to reach them.

Paul Gorski (2006) echoes Paulo Freire's work from *The Pedagogy of Indignation* by succinctly defining the concept of deficit thinking as a way of

> identifying deficiencies in the cultures and behaviors of some identity group. They blame oppressed people for their oppression by ignoring systemic inequities and drawing on stereotypes already established in the mainstream consciousness. Deficit theory has been discredited by decades of research revealing that people in poverty have similar aspirations and values as economically privileged people and that the disadvantages they face result from injustice, not personal deficiency. (Gorski, 2006)

Past literature of African-American student achievement (Baratz & Baratz, 1970) espoused a deficit view of such children, identified for what they lacked—whether it is proper nutrition, proper parenting, lives free from the threat of violence, the absence of resource, access to books or bountiful verbal stimulation. In this mind set, teachers see students as needing fixing, as having something wrong with them, having limitations based on the absences that exist in their lives that we, as instructors, feel duty-bound to protect in the form of lowered expectations. This belief has damaged generations of children. Teachers in this mind set believe students cannot truly learn because of the social ills infecting them. The predominance of non-standard English in students' daily verbal and written use is used as a sign of student limitation. This perception feeds lowered expectations that fosters a deepening spiral of limited opportunity and lost learning perpetuated by teachers themselves. Our ignorance or blindness to the depth and sophistication of the talents minority students hold retard our ability as teachers to reach. Those who do remove themselves from their own cultural base and look at students through their cultural strengths have a better chance of seeing their students as potential-filled, not potential-averse. Research in cultural diversity acceptance has shown that "successful teachers of African-American children tend to be connected with their students' communities, possess insider knowledge of children's cultural worlds, and use this information to help children construct new knowledge" (Lazar et al., 2006).

Lazar et al. (2006) tested this theory in a study of teachers in the Philadelphia public schools. These teachers were surveyed about their perceptions of their own culture, their students' cultures, the type of communities in which the teachers resided and the extent to which they used their knowledge about the cultures of their students in their planning. Their findings patterned the challenges presented in deficit thinking in reference to students. "Most of the European-American, suburban . . . [teachers] framed their descriptions of children's culture around what the children lacked with respect to the dominant culture. These teachers emphasized poverty and non-traditional family structures as factors that played a significant role in children's out-of-school lives" (Lazar et al., 2006). The primary description by these teachers of the behaviors of their students was "deviant" as pertains to the predominant culture. Other African-American (and some European-American teachers), conversely, described their students in terms of *what they have* rather than *what they lack*. While recognizing the circumstances their students live and contend with as being unfortunate or sad, they did not use those circumstances to consign their students to a lower level of achievement. These teachers recognized their students' love of music and incorporated music in their teaching. They noted their students socializing skills as positive elements. They did not view their students in terms of pathological absences and deficits that are unassailable or insurmountable.

See your students as they are and for what they possess. Enter into their culture to see what they know and value and use that value to connect them to the learning you wish them to acquire. This beats the "bar held high" approach with you as the taskmaster looking down and deriding them until they attempt to reach your perceptions or give up in frustration. But do not fall into the "they can only learn so much" limiting approach either that presents unnatural and deficit anchors on their learning. Stretching with them is more potentially beneficial than seeing them as unfortunate products of a deformed and deficient minority culture. Perpetuate that thinking, and you continue to be a part of the problem.

CHAPTER TWELVE

A Pep Talk About Parents

Your Partners and the Obstacles and the Potential Lessons Within Your Interaction With Them

W hy don't they address the subject of "parents" in teacher school? Among the subjects that mystify and confound yet has the strongest potential to reaching students is the relationship you develop with the parents of your students. Yet the subject rarely surfaces in teacher preparation.

The first thing to remember is that what you do in the classroom is reflected back in the home by students in some way. If you're perceived as cool, you're gushed about; if mean and unfair, they'll carp. The sentences you say will be retranslated into family-speak. If you want to meet the parents but refuse to be proactive about it, you'll never see them. You may have a lineup of parents and not have the ones you really want to see show up. You may have parents who are angry, intoxicated, fearful and shy come to see you. You may even have parents hit on you one time, as my daughter attests, with a child in tow! You definitely have to create your own protocol for working with parents.

Acknowledgment: The author thanks Nancy Northrip for her insights and experience in shaping this chapter.

For soon-to-be-teachers, it's helpful to imagine your students with you in your classroom by a see-through wall where their parents sit and observe, obsess, and worry about how their children are doing. For young teachers, the prospect of dealing with parents mystifies and even evokes anxiety. These are people, who for the most part, are older and at a place where most young teachers have yet to traverse. They can intimidate or frustrate, and a plan of action and understanding is as important with them as it is with your students, especially if you wish to establish a powerful learning team with them as allies with a similar mission. Some thoughts on doing that:

BECOMING STUDENTS OF YOUR STUDENTS AND THEIR PARENTS

It would help to see your task as learning about the parents of your students as part of the challenge. Becoming a student of your students' parents is an unusual goal to recommend. So frequently, teachers in schools see parents as part of the problem, as obstacles to student improvement. Teachers frequently make the mistake of seeing themselves as the professionals in learning and regard parents in a lesser light. I say reverse that dynamic. If you look upon the parents of your students as experts on their children, and your role partly learning from them as much as helping to acquire their alliance on behalf of the students, you may have something powerful upon which to build. Frequently, parents are seen as oblivious to the challenges facing students. Some teachers, especially veteran teachers, evince superiority in the belief that they can see who students really are, and what parents see only is an amalgam of denial and blindness. I believe many parents are more deeply attuned to their children than parents of an older generation might have been. While students who come from low-income family situations deal with stresses associated with what poverty provides, still there are parents savvy enough to know what makes their children tick—what motivates them as well as what doesn't work with them. Why would you not want to align yourself with such knowledge, learn from them as you learn from their children as part of the process to see what the children need and what is getting in their way?

KNOWLEDGE OF PARENTS COMES
IN A COMPLICATED PACKAGE

Still, it is important to understand that a parent who enters the school or engages with the teacher as an expert on their child also brings to that table a set of their own issues. The package of knowledge you seek from your students' parents also comes with complicated packaging. Parents may project to you their anxieties about parenting. They may be beset with their own personal issues, work strife, marital distress, and these may color the conversation or be revealed once parents sense you are an advocate on their side. They may bring their own anxieties about school itself, may be unnecessarily defensive or timid or overprotective because they are projecting their own school experiences into the conversation.

If these circumstances arise, the best stance to take is nonjudgmental acceptance. If concerned parents come to contact you, the concern may be complicated by other worries they may have about their children or about their lives. Frequently this may be discovered with a simple question such as, "Is this the only issue that is bothering you today?" What you get in response may be beyond your pay grade, as the saying goes, but can sharpen the best skill you can have in working with the parents of your students.

LISTEN. LISTEN. LISTEN.

Active engaged listening is an important skill in working with parents. They must sense you are deeply trying to understand them. Some techniques from communication skills are presented here:

Mirroring

The practice of repeating what you hear in an attempt to acquire clarity has been parodied as a dubious process of counseling. Still, it helps to present a person in accepting mode trying to understand the nature of the parents' concern. A parent once came to me with the concern, "The B you gave to my son will prevent him from going to Princeton." My response: "You're saying that the B I gave your son . . . (pause. Repeat the "I gave" to distinguish

from the "he earned" which would be part of the discussion later.)
The conversation moved from the esoteric distinctions between
giving and earning to other questions. Did the student want to go
to Princeton? Is one grade from one marking period in one class
on one report card truly the determining factor in acceptance
or denial enrollment practices at Princeton? Back to the previous
question—who is it that wants the student to go to Princeton?
Mirroring helps to clarify the point while possibly revealing the
subsidiary points.

Feel. Felt. Found.

This technique suggests the following three-part response:

- Validate the perspective of the parent:"I understand how you
  must feel in this circumstance."
- Assuage worry by asserting that the parent is not alone in their
  feelings:"Others have felt similarly in this circumstance." and
- Suggest that the school proper has discovered some example
  things that can help: "We have found that this circumstance
  can be eased in this manner."

Sympathy Properly Expressed

The teacher succeeds with parents by showing a sincere attempt
to understand and empathize with their concerns. The goal is to convey that you and the parent are part of the team, and not that you are
trying to show the parent is wrong or silly in what is thought. A
valuable question if appropriate, especially when talking about
student behavior that needs improving is, "Tell me how you handle
this at home." Your work will be seen as an extension of theirs, validating what they feel and know about their child, and presenting
the possibility of alliance, together improving the educational experience. Do not offer sympathy diluted by disagreement or disbelief.
Their concerns have legitimacy because they are concerned.
Empathy and understanding are the first steps towards reconcilia-
tion and plan of action, with partnership establishing and strengthening the ultimate goal.

YOUR VERY STANCE WILL HELP

How you convey sincerity with your students' parents extends to how you look to them. Do not remain behind the big desk if meeting them. Sit alongside them as equals and do not present a version of the teacher-student separation. Most important—look them in the eye at all times. Do not hold your arms crossed in defensive or accusatory mode. Open your stance, open your eyes, and look to place yourself as equal partner rather than managing partner.

CALMING THE ANGER

Parents contact the teacher frequently in anger or distress over a circumstance. The potential volatility of the encounter requires strong thought and a plan in order to become a positive experience. These steps help:

- Listening openly as they vent
- Sympathizing by validating their concerns
- Seeking solution through consult with superiors in the building
- Promising response and proposing resolution by end of the following day

The last of these suggestions may be the most difficult to acquire. Parents who take the time to visit or call in anger may demand immediate resolution, and the circumstances may require some thinking at the moment. It is preferable to have resolution outside the realm of anger, however. If you promise a resolution by a certain time, honor that promise.

It also helps to avoid being defensive. This is also difficult to achieve when confronted by an angry parent, for the immediate response resides in our fight or flight instinct. The message here is not to be defensive nor rise to the level of heat being presented to you.

There is nothing wrong with a sincere apology. Whatever the source of the tumult, whatever else going on in the parent's mind or life is additional to the conversation. An upset parent is upset for a reason, and you can sympathize properly with that upset. How well you resolve the upset is determined by how you react to the meeting—therefore, the need to plan.

So you see it helps to see parents as partners in your effort and not obstacles. From that stance, seek them out with introductory letters before school starts. Give them messages, call or e-mail when their child does something well, as well as when they press on your sensitive buttons. The parent may not give you permission to "whack them," as a couple of parents memorably advised me thirty years ago. They may ask you about parenting skills, especially challenging if you have not reached that vaunted stage of your life yet. Though note this irony—how better you get at teaching when you become Mom or Dad. Few things improved my teaching ability more than becoming a parent. You develop such empathy and understanding of the stresses parenthood holds.

So look at parents as partners who can help you reach your students. Take a proactive stance with them and show them the extent of your care. As a parent, I gravitated to the teachers of my children who evinced a "we're all in this together for the sake of your baby" approach, while those with the "my way or the highway" attitude received my mental write off.

Of course, you will not please them all, and again I wish universities would give some time to preparing you to work with the ones who have plaintive anger in their voices. I never returned the anger, which is one really good piece of advice, and I would watch what I would say to students because of the reinterpretation that could occur with student translation. But standing your ground when you believe you have acted accordingly (and not in a doctrinaire fashion) is advisable.

These moments with parents can be indelible. I ran into a dad whose son I taught twenty years earlier, and he greeted me with exactly the first line I said to him at parent's night about his boy. Isn't that amazing? Like students, parents also can retain a kindness extended or injustice visited upon their child years afterward. My children have recounted their teachers from kindergarten on and praise or dismiss them with a telling remembrance. Truth be told—I do that as well in recounting their teachers.

In summation, exuding with parents a sense that you understand their children, seek their knowledge about them, hold faith in both parent and student, and cheerlead their way across childhood and adolescence—these markers will fill your students and their parents with regard and reverence for your work. Seem to not care, take an aggressive and unforgiving stance with them, and prepare for ninja battle.

Most teachers dread the phone message from parents. I say take the opposite tack. You are a licensed problem solver. You will have problems requiring solving. This I never could understand about our colleagues. Some expect or hope or dodge themselves into circumstances to have as few problems as possible. Why? Your job is to diagnose. To do that—you need problems. I say relish the fact that you have problems, some of which can be resolved with parental assistance! Your solutions will be many-layered with short- and long-term effect. Some times your prognoses will be questioned. Welcome parents with questions and doubts and concerns whether packaged in anger or fear. Seek to allay their concerns and ally them on behalf of their children.

REFLECTIVE EXERCISE

Activity

- Set up a plan of action for working with parents. Role-play. Consider multiple modes (angry parent, supportive parent, parent with ancillary worries) and role-play how you would respond to different parent behaviors.
- Ask a colleague to see a representative sample of communication with a parent to learn about more effective phrasing. There are always better ways of phrasing student behavior that would draw parents to you as an ally rather than away from you as a defender.

CHAPTER THIRTEEN

Seven Yin-Yang Blunders to Avoid in the Early Years of Teaching

Most students of Shakespeare (2009) see the depiction of Polonius, the worry-wart father of the hot blooded Laertes in *Hamlet* as a buffoon worthy of snicker. Always fretting about his son's desire to be out on his own in the world, Polonius offers to his boy seemingly contradictory advice on acting neither one way nor another:

> *Give thy thoughts no tongue,*
>
> *Nor any unproportioned thought his act.*
>
> *Be thou familiar, but by no means vulgar. . . .*
>
> *Give every man thy ear, but few thy voice;*
>
> *Take each man's censure, but reserve thy judgment.*
>
> *Neither a borrower nor a lender be. . . .*

A seeming bundle of contradictions lies here. So do this, but be sure to do the opposite: don't fight, but if you get into one, kick butt; listen, but don't speak. Huh? Most student depictions of the son listening to the father show Laertes rolling his eyes at his father's seemingly endless prattle.

But be careful in teaching, for things are often not one way or the other. You look for absolutes, and there are very few besides the bawdy and the obvious, such as: *Never hit your students. Always be clothed when in front of them. Never tell them they're stupid.* But there are early-year blunders in teaching when it is wise to seek middle ground and not be one thing or the other exclusively. Here are some yin-yangs that come to mind:

- Teach with passion, but don't teach with passion alone.
- Don't teach as you were taught, but don't teach as if they can't learn.
- Know why you're up there and where you're going, but be prepared to go a different way.
- Do not be afraid of silence or noise, and do not speak when you should listen.
- Do not be a slave to coverage, but do not belabor.
- Do not seek control of the classroom but do not relinquish command of it.
- Know a great deal about a subject, but don't lord it, get them to seek it.

There are more and there are nuances those years of experience will reveal to you, but let's have you focus on just avoiding these early on.

TEACH WITH PASSION, BUT DON'T TEACH WITH PASSION ALONE

Nothing moves students more than the sense that their teacher is animated and excited about that which is taught, except for their sense that the teacher expresses care and concern. A person drawn to the subject who seeks the best way to present with understanding and verve has a good chance of reaching students. You have to have a deep understanding of your subject in order to know how best to present to students without boring them or losing them or forgetting their presence.

Ordinarily, your knowledge base and your emotion should combine to present both concern for those in front of you and concern that you are presenting the body of knowledge well, in a manner that allows students to enter and relax their natural inclination to disbelieve both teacher and message. There is a middle ground that makes you neither the whirling dervish of nothing nor the mirthless Yoda. You must find that middle ground and improve thereby.

Don't Teach as You Were Taught, but Don't Teach as if They Can't Learn

My, this is a common foible. You are the product of those who inspired you to teach. You reveled in the way in which the subject was presented and you see yourself as the natural heir of that teaching excellence. You enter the classroom and teach as if your room is full of mini-you's, all ready to catch the fire you caught. Then when it doesn't happen as it happened to you—what will you do? You will feel momentary vertigo—I loved this stuff back then—it turned me on to learning and gave me direction. What gives? What gives is the student you were is not in front of you. It's somewhat analogous to returning to your old high school a year or so later to feel that vague sense of displacement. The place has the same bricks and the same faces within, but where was that spirit in which you thrived? It left when you flung your square, tasseled cap in the air. The high school you had is not the one in which you returned. The same thing occurs with those in front of you. They are not you, they have not the life arc you traversed. It would be as if you expect they would have the same taste in music and art as you. *No—you are not in them; you must seek who they are.*

Face the reality in front of you, but do not ever believe they cannot achieve. Lift the bar, and your game, and find the middle ground that will move them more forward than they ever have been moved before.

Know Why You're Up There and Where You're Going, but Be Prepared to Go a Different Way

Worksheets are not going to do it. The back of an envelope filled with questions will not move the earth either. This is the major blunder to avoid. You must plan, plan, plan. Your day has a reason that connects to what will occur tomorrow and what hearkens back to yesterday's event. You have lessons connected to a unit, units connected to a theme, themes that present a framework of your tenets. You may be given a curriculum, you may be given a syllabus, but the curriculum does not teach itself. If it did, your presence would be superfluous. If it did, you could get the former paramour who broke your heart to come in and teach while you sit in the back of the room wondering what went wrong. The curriculum has to be animated by a framework that is your responsibility to devise. Today can't be just a paean to the thing being done today, in isolation from days preceding or since. Your question can not serve only (you would fervently hope) to get three minutes closer to the end of class. There must be a decided plan of approach to every question, every assignment, every decision, and every action you initiate as a professional educator. Action without purpose is as easily detectable to a student as dancing without talent. Six-year-olds who cannot articulate the phrase "winging it" will sense a lack of cohesion and purpose in classroom activities even if you tried to browbeat them into submission with histrionics and teacher-saber rattling (the loud voice, the vague threat of punishment, both which I have seen in elementary school teachers, and where is the gulag where such can be consigned?). You must, you absolutely must know where you are going with your students.

Yet there lies a deep yang to this teaching yin. I had a poetry professor who would stymie me with his logic that a poet must learn all that can be learned about the subject of the poem and be prepared to abandon all of what was learned to enter the poem. Huh? Of course, this same professor was more often than not found to be discussing with unknown and presumed angelic voices in the quad during a rain fall (this in the age before cell phones, where now everyone seems to be in deep conversation with their imaginary friends), so I thought his injunction was just part of his celestial running conversation. That is until I entered teaching and discovered that the plan is always subservient to the students for whom the plan was devised, and if there lies a path desired by the students to traverse, plan be damned! Follow that line and see if it can be drawn back to the plan you had *if* you are lucky enough to garner their interest, mine that field as if golden. You may not catch on, but true and decent learning is going on in those moments, and sometimes you are not there to generate it as much as you are to observe and air traffic control it to allow everyone the chance to speak.

Do Not Be Afraid of Silence or Noise, and Do Not Speak When You Should Listen

People, Americans especially, seem uncomfortable in silence and fretful about noise. We want to burst in applause during the symphony during the silence between movements, and no rock concerts' softer moment can exist without the plaintive whistle or the doped-crazed cry. A moment of dead time on television has us fumbling angrily for the remote, and conversations around any dinner table become stilted in the presence of pause. We love sound, pretty much any sound unaccompanied by pain (and even then, as my perpetually whistling ears attest, I did love getting painfully close to Neil Young and Crazy Horse's wail in "Hurricane" and sat in the front row of Led Zeppelin at their peak, while the opening chords of "Kashmir" brought me tinnitus—my constantly present companion). What we do fret about is silence. We're a bit like pheasants who only squawk and flee when the crunching of snow stops. So in our classrooms we're conscious of a false corollary—time only passes in a classroom with sound and learning only occurs with human voice to propel it. The new teacher will do or say pretty much anything to get the silence to stop—answer the question asked, plea for a nice student's rescue, pile questions atop each other until they crumble around each other like a *Blues Brothers* police car pile-up. Students get nervous too. In the hum of classroom noise students can fiddle, stare, speak in desultory tones under the radar. But in silence everyone gets edgy. The natural order seems awry.

I often took a Zen approach to still moments in the classroom. If the question asked was worth answering it's worth letting it steep awhile. Now if the question was stupid or awkwardly phrased, students will give you the *huh?* sign and you can regroup. But like still moments in the theater a still classroom moment may have its own meaning.

But when they talk, the last person who should be talking is you. Responding to student response is an art form. Learning how to get out of the way of your students' learning is the surest sign you are progressing as an educator. If the opportunity presents itself, watch a teacher you admire work and examine the way questions are asked, silenced orchestrated, and discussions led. True artisans know that less is more when it comes to teacher banter. You know you're smart, went to college, read and wrote, and thought the great ideas. But when they are talking, stem your urge to opine.

The same thought should go into student noise. The common myth is that the noisy classroom of the new teacher is the classroom in trouble. Student engagement is a sign you are reaching them—but then there is productive noise that is the approach to understanding and the subtextual noise that is the replay of the fight at the party on Saturday. Know the difference between the noise that furthers your class framework from the one that furthers the distance between that which they know and that which they could know. We get lazy when we do not distinguish. Sometimes teachers use the wave of student sound to allow them to finish what they need to do—the paperwork, the answering of student questions, or, in one egregious moment I witnessed, completing the application of lotion to one's legs (and you can trust that need not be done during class time. Dry skin is not terminal.) Noise and silence are the coda of the classroom. Learning to distinguish between the extremes of both furthers your classroom acumen.

Do Not Be a Slave to Coverage, but Do Not Belabor

The only timetable you truly have to be concerned about is the timetable of your students' hearts and heads. Moving them along a curriculum requires you to be part seer and part defender. It makes no sense at all to whisk through material for the sake of being aligned with every other teacher teaching that grade or subject. That kind of lockstep unanimity appeals to administrators given their desire for uniform approach to material, so if a student needs to move out of one class into another, there is little catch up to do. That's strictly administrative hogwash, for it presupposes you lord over automatons in classrooms who learn at the same rate while teachers present at the same rate. The notion is antithetic to what should predominate in classroom decisions. So if you are getting pressured about not being where everyone else is, resist the attempt to make the comment an embedded criticism of your work. At the same time, marshal your own pace so you can be sure you're not taking baby steps with the curriculum when students could stride more confidently. The students will follow your lead. If they sense you are slowing down for reasons unassociated with them they'll pick up on it and slow down with you—in the form of the whine and the sigh. Your gauge of whether they are handling the material sufficiently to go onward must include being attuned to their propensity to slow curricular movement. If you ever had a personal trainer you know your tendency when his or her back is turned—you ease up when not under the watchful eye. Sometimes teachers slow classes down because they themselves are not ready to move on—oftentimes for reasons unassociated with the students. Perhaps all the essays have not been read, or the syllabus forthcoming has not been completed. Maybe your personal life has gone awry, and you have needed to spend time repairing, repining, or repenting. You must try to keep those pauses down to a minimum. You rush through the curriculum; you hurt them and solve nothing. You take too much time on one subject, aspect, and unit or lesson—ditto.

DO NOT SEEK CONTROL OF THE CLASSROOM, BUT DO NOT RELINQUISH COMMAND OF IT

This issue of command and control in the classroom is tricky, needing the new teacher to understand clearly the dynamic of a classroom and how best to begin its establishment and not fall prey to pitfall and error that would lead to further error in correction.

The legitimacy of your presence in the classroom in your mind is seated in the trust the school has placed in you. You have the keys, the grade book, the sharp clothes, and the presence as the sole adult in the classroom. The students you meet have none of those parameters in their minds as they regard your entrance. To them you have been placed in a mental temporary limbo. You are regarded with the same bland well-let's-see-what-this-one-has-to-offer tissue-thin veneer of regard and obeisance. They are there because more powerful forces compel their presence and quietude. They are there out of a vague sense of curiosity. They are there because their friends are nearby or practice is soon. They are there because high school or college beckons and they retain some hope that things will improve in school and in their lives. They are there because they wish not to face the fact they truly have nowhere else to go and they retain the sense that out-of-school time is more risky, seedy, and sad. They will abandon their veneer of regard for you, and here is the inner irony of classroom dynamic, *when they receive a clear sign from you that it is OK to do so.* The onus is on you to establish a classroom atmosphere that will compel them to continue, behave, and achieve. The stance that you take is the very essence of the yin-yang quality I have tried to express in this chapter. Be a taskmaster and things will work but only for a short time. Attempt to be their friend and things will work, but only for a short time. The balance you strike will resonate with the quality and depth of the framework of the lessons that you have crafted beforehand and you will refine them into a more sound fashion when you understand your students and their needs. Your presentation of yourself as someone with something of value for them is something that they may sense. The depth of your talent admixed with your concern will transcend the subject you teach. At the very best level of practice, your work will allow your students to approach the clarity of the identity they seek for themselves. You use humor well, surprising them by abandoning the "no smiling until the winter" idiocy past teacher preparers have warned. It will surface when the bold try their initial games to play on you—the hyperactive or the ones close to giving up on the usefulness of school will try to establish their dominance by showing their classmates your limitations and camouflage of concern. How you handle these testing moments will emit a half-life resonance with them. This is a teacher who knows what she is doing. This is a teacher comfortable in her own skin and comfortable in the presence of young people.

In my teaching years, I railed about the value of the opening paragraphs of essays as the opportunity to show the reader that the writer has a comfortable command of what was learned in the exercise and lays out a path by which the reader can follow and understand how the writer acquired that perspective. The opening days of the school year are the first paragraphs of the essay you create with your students. Errors in logic and absence of clarity confound the efforts later on in the school year. The difference in this analogy is that while the teacher knows where she wishes to go and conveys that confidence, the teacher has yet one more vital task to complete—the study of the students in front of her. Only with that knowledge will the teacher refine and improve that which has been framed and planned. The essay writer has but one audience—the reader, as different as the stars but gathered together only by immutable words on the page. The teacher lives in a vibrant place where the understanding of audience is crucial to the degree of success attained. The classroom dynamic approaches the analog of composing an essay on the spot over time, all the while looking at the audience, altering the format to try and acquire the effect on each member of the audience despite their limitations and despite their misgivings. The success of your work will result in students moving you in their minds past the limbo they place you to another mental place—either as a teacher of impact and merit or a teacher of moment. The latter is withstood, disregarded, and forgotten. The former has the opportunity to move students toward further understanding themselves, their direction, and their purpose. The former brings students to an understanding of the transcendent qualities of subject taught well by a guide and a champion.

Your success depends on how you transcend the rank the front office bestowed on you to present your students a command of purpose, regard, and self-knowledge. In the absence of command lies the seeds of the permission you give your students to dismiss you, long before you give them the OK that class is dismissed.

KNOW A GREAT DEAL ABOUT YOUR SUBJECT, BUT DON'T LORD IT OVER THEM; GET THEM TO SEEK IT

Every teacher true to his or her roots will admit knowledge of any subject only deepened under the pressure of teaching that subject. Early in my career, my command of grammar was pedestrian at best. I was great at moving students with what I was saying and writing and pretty good at getting them to improve their writing, but my command of the terminology was only toughened in the context of teaching. In rhetorical technique, tense and case, gerunds and participles, I was limited. My teacher preparation in English soared on the theme, but soured on the rhetoric, and I had to double-time to learn while determining how best to present to students. That kind of exhaustion is frequent in young teachers, without a depth of subject knowledge, learning on the fly and flying to find the right way to present.

So you are certainly better off knowing deeply your subject, but its limitation is if you walk in as if you're Kung-Fu Master and your students are Grasshoppers, and their task is to first discover how little they know in the presence of your brilliance and then work like heck to get enough knowledge to merit your grudging grunt.

Being the person with all the answers does not help them much, for if you present that image, then your classes become the limited game of finding out what teacher knows. If your goal is to show them how brilliant you are, then their work is all focused on getting a yes or a nod from you.

What is more dimensional is positioning your knowledge in such a way that the students sense that together you are exploring and considering. My science colleagues steeped in the inquiry science method are great with this technique. They'll put together a circumstance that is amazing—note in a vat of water that Coke cans sink and Diet Coke cans float (try it). Now why would that be, they query, and the answers come flying—heavier ink, presence of sugar in one and not the other   cans of different weight, thickness, or construction. Well lookie here, they counter—purchased ice from the store is clear but ice from your fridge is not—now why is that? And the kids go batty with theory and supposition. From a stance of curiosity, kids test theories and suppositions while the teacher steadfastly refuses to explain the answer. Instead, the teacher encourages inquiry—testing of theory. It's only half like magic, only the magician's stance is curious wonder and the inclination to entice students to figure it out. How much cooler is that as technique rather than just showing off your knowledge by telling and lecturing and posturing?

Such a technique elicits the value and strength of generative questions, where the inquiry is seated in the questions seeking not as much a quick and thought limiting answer as the resolution of a mystery with multiple possibilities.

PART III

Staying There

Chapter Fourteen

Classroom Ethics

68 What-If's That Will Make Any Teacher Say "Yikes!"

How long do you think it will take for this kind of moment to happen to you? A circumstance will occur in your classroom or in the school or in the cafeteria or faculty lounge, and you will pause a moment and think to yourself, "You know, college never prepared me for handling this!" You will exit your traditional teacher preparation program at the fine University of Wherever with their good wishes, but unless the place is extraordinary in its devotion to aftercare, you will receive scant assistance or mentoring thereafter. You will arrive with your mile-wide, inch-deep command of subject matter, your limited knowledge of children, and your still incomplete knowledge of yourself. The series of maps carefully constructed in your mind and heart will now enter the territory of your own classroom. Finally, you have your walls (if you're lucky enough not to share rooms), your grade book, your children, and your responsibility to heal or harm or do nothing. Then you begin, and within seconds of beginning, I daresay, you will come across a moment that you have not prepared yourself to encounter. For most new teachers, these are not usually aha moments of sudden discovery. These

Acknowledgments: The author thanks Peg Cain for permission to use her *what-if* game in this chapter. The author also thanks David Ripley for permission to use the situations he crafted for ethics discussion in his School Law course.

are likelier to be moments that elicit a *Yikes!* or a *What?* or almost certainly a *Help!*

Every teacher who has passed through the traditional pathway has tales of the chasm that exists between the experiences of traditional preparation and the real-life responsibilities of the teaching profession. I recall with the nostalgia only experience can provide my first English department chair. He was a courtly and deeply decent man, who gave me in July the textbooks I needed to review for my first year's teaching assignment. All summer long, I studied those textbooks and planned the dickens out of how I would approach the first unit, writing down my questions for the lessons to come on the backs of business-size envelopes. On my first day, I discovered that my colleague had given me the wrong texts. What he had described as a remedial class was in fact a college-bound one, and vice versa. I could hear in my mind Clint Eastwood in the movie *Heartbreak Ridge* shouting, "You're a Marine: you adapt, you improvise, and you overcome." Well, I was *no* Marine, and at the time it seemed likelier that my teacher preparation had been a prelude to my true career in improvisational comedy.

During my very first week of teaching, a young girl came up to me to ask if she could go to the bathroom. As she asked, her thumb slipped under one of the buttons of her blouse and flicked the button into my face. Before I could respond to that surprise, the young girl collapsed into a seizure in front of me. I had never seen a seizure before. I had no idea what to do. My first impulse was to clear the classroom. Why? I had no idea. "Everyone get out of here!" I shouted. The students were happy to oblige, and in an instant twenty-four young people under my responsibility were out roaming the halls.

My second impulse was to try to pick the girl up and carry her to the nurse's office. Have you ever contended with the strength of someone in seizure? She quickly swatted me aside. I was grateful that a colleague wondering why students were wandering the halls poked her head in, grasped the situation, and pressed the call button. Call button? What's that, I wondered?

That moment, one of my very first as a professional educator, clearly showed that my college had helped prepare me to do a fine job explaining how a poem worked but had offered me nothing at all on what to do when a student convulsed. And at that moment, knowing about convulsions was much more important to me than poetry.

Twelve Classroom Situations

Welcome to the learning curve! Perhaps as student teachers or as novice teachers you noticed that you were in a double bind. You didn't know the material coming in, yet you still had to prepare a lesson to impart what you yourself had barely learned. So how could you notice, let alone act upon, the multiple cues, teachable moments, and subtextual messages your students were sending with their questions or their body language or their silence? And where would you find the resources to respond when a moment came up that had no reference to the lesson plan at hand or to literature, science, or any college course or law school course you'd ever taken?

The bulk of teaching occurs in the multitude of decisions you will make in reaction to circumstances you had not anticipated encountering. Those decisions, the ones you are forced to make when you are unsure, distracted, or overburdened, will determine the quality of your teaching, just as the measure of your teaching will derive not from the students who love you but from the ones who most challenge. This is why operating under a set of tenets will help you, because when situations arise causing you to enter a *yikes* moment, your principles will be there to guide you.

What makes these situations so vexing is that they're often not curricular. When I visited methodology classes with prospective teachers, they bombarded me with, "What do you do when?" questions. Those new teachers didn't want to talk about how Madeline Hunter (1994) had transformed instructional practice. They wanted to talk about the young Maddie Hunters in their classrooms, the students who were providing those extracurricular *yikes* moments. Those moments arise not only when working with your students but also with their parents, with administrators, with colleagues, with the central office, and with board members. The new teacher is often exhausted for very good reason.

A systematic approach to these untoward situations would take up an entire text in and of itself. If you are lucky, the veteran teacher who befriends and mentors you will also give you instruction in the culture of your school community, allowing you to laugh with him or her in the recounting of errors made and life lessons learned. The following scenarios are memorable ones for me because they happened during my teaching career, when I erred as often as I chose correctly in the decisions I made. Perhaps they can serve as preamble to one of the great challenges you will encounter in your teaching career: teaching-situation ethics.

> 1. A student writes in a journal or essay perspectives that could be construed as suicidal. Or a student confides in you that he or she has considered suicide. You are the only person this student has told about these feelings. The student pleads with you to keep the conversations confidential because the student fears shame, anger, or recrimination that would be too much to bear if you divulge the problem to others.

We so focus on student feelings today that this scenario should offer no challenge to you, but as a young teacher it vexed me considerably. In my "I can change the world one person at a time" stage, I kept the confidence of a disturbed student, to my deep distress. The result was one evening I received a phone call at home from this student, who had slashed her wrists and was calling in a dim haze from a phone booth. She described nearby landmarks, allowing me to visualize where she was, and there I went in my car on a Saturday night to bring a bleeding and disoriented student to my home, where my wife and I bandaged her. Whatever was I thinking?

In a subsequent call to her therapist, he made it very clear that I the unwitting fool was not helping her in the least. Still I was surprised when this student's next act was to tape a suicide note to my front door. I recall the absolute frustration of being so out of my league, so thoroughly exhausted by the mental anguish of working with her sadness, that for a moment I thought to myself, "All right, die then!" as I read her taped note. But then I went in and called the police. Fortunately she was found before tragedy occurred, she received the help she needed, and she recovered and moved on with her life.

That's the amazing thing sometimes. If a professional can intervene in time with students who can't see through their unhappy today to the promise of tomorrow, odds are those students will recover well.

If such an event happens to you, tell everyone! Make copies and distribute them to counselor, principal, psychologist, and department chair. Law now forces our hand, making teachers liable if such steps are not heeded. Allow those trained in such matters to assist. The child may very well be giving you permission to tell everyone by telling you. Risking losing someone's trust is worth the effort. It is far better to lose that trust than to stare at that child's casket searching your memory for cues about what you might have done better or faster. In this circumstance, you act upon the principle that you are not an island nor are you the only person on the earth who can help someone. That lone rebel image of the teacher portrayed by Robin Williams in *Dead Poet's Society* is dangerous. When you start to think you are the only person in the building who really cares about your students, you will start to err.

> 2. You notice a student of yours with whom you are on good terms in close physical contact with another student of the same gender. In the teacher's lounge, some of your colleagues comment about having witnessed such activity. What if anything do you do?

Here your own moral code may conflict with your good sense and place you in a position to err. The problem surfaces when you do not delay judgment. Remember, what seems is often not what is. Further, what right do you have to pass judgment over the sexual proclivities of your students, unless those students' activities are marring the educational climate of your room?

In this circumstance, a well-intentioned colleague felt honor bound to pull one of the students in this scenario aside to warn her that her reputation can be harmed if she engaged in this kind of immoral activity. This student immediately came to interrupt a meeting I was having with a colleague to tearfully demand if any more of our colleagues were discussing her moral stature. This was followed next day by a meeting with the students and her attorney father, broadly intimating that this teacher's words were *actionable*, a phrase I hope you never have to hear in your career. What a mess! This entire trauma originated from a decision to make a moralistic judgment. Hayakawa (1949/1991) wrote of the dangers of such decisions he called inferences, statements of the unknown made on the basis of the known. While exceedingly valuable to use in developing our insight and sensitivity, relying on inferences to make judgments can lead us astray. We note the student dressed in a manner our perceptions would deem slovenly and may infer any of a number of conclusions, most of them wrong, about such a person. In the realm of students' interpersonal relationships, our perceptions often are the victims of our incomplete knowledge. But the overriding question to ask yourself is what business it is of yours to comment on your students' sexuality?

Consider how you would respond to this similar scenario.

> 3. A student confides in you that he or she believes she is not hetero-sexual but isn't sure and seeks your advice.

This scenario has all the markings of "they never told me how to handle this in college." You may have gained the trust and respect of a student who seeks words from you on a subject you may find personally immoral if not distasteful. Now you certainly can brush the student off by claiming you don't talk about personal matters and that will clear your responsibility from further concern. But do your instincts lead you to such a callous response? Do you want to pontificate, quote Biblical passages, and warn the student of the damnation to come from wandering away from sexual orthodoxy? Well, that might assuage your sense of righteousness, but do you see yourself engaging in such dogmatism? But are you also uncomfortable embracing homo-sexuality or encouraging further experimentation? Do you see yourself as a proselytizer for alternative lifestyles?

Any way you go, this one is a difficult call. Why do you think a student might confide such a thing to you? What would that student be hoping for from you? If you think *acceptance,* you may have something. The student may be struggling with a matter that requires intense personal reflection. If that student has high regard for you, losing that regard would be harmful. Maybe the best thing you could tell that student is that your own regard for people does not center on a personal matter such as sexual orientation.

You can admit that you admire this student; you will continue to admire this student. I have always contended that the most silent minority in the school setting, the most isolated and the most aggrieved, is the gay high school student. You may not wish to advance the gay lifestyle, and that is fine, but you need not harangue against it either.

How many students do you think teachers have lost because we did not offer understanding and acceptance of the students' true selves, regardless of the challenges confronting them? Why would any one of us want to continue any young person's pain?

In such cases, it does matter if you accept your students and they sense your acceptance. The price of your regard should not be their adherence to your own version of morality and righteousness.

> 4. A student asks your advice on where to obtain an abortion.

Would your response depend on your own opinion about abortion? Should you give in to the temptation to launch into a pro-life or pro-choice diatribe? Should you give this student the advice requested? What might happen if the student followed your advice— say obtained an abortion at a place you recommended and then discovered it was against the opinion of her parents who were now looking to you for redress of their grievance? What if you counseled a student to keep a child against the wishes of her family? Is it your place to offer such advice, or is it more appropriate to serve as a resource directing her to the person(s) who are more appropriate to offer such advice?

This is one of those circumstances when you must realize that you are part of a larger educational community devoted to helping all of the children in that community. This student may have come to you because she trusts you, but that does not mean this student should trust only you. As part of an educational community, you are still helping your students even if you ask for help. The teacher who is a lone wolf may look romantic, but that kind of romance is high risk.

> 5. A student asks if you have and can offer (a) a breath mint, (b) a pain reliever (aspirin, ibuprofen), (c) a feminine napkin/tampon.

Most of us will rightfully see the dangers inherent in giving students any kind of medication, not knowing if the student has allergies or other conditions that could be aggravated by that medication. Breath mints may be relatively harmless, but there are some schools that will advise you never to offer anyone anything, while other schools have classrooms stocked with tissue boxes and other supplies free and open for students to use. When a student during summer school asked me if I had any tampons, she clearly was a student in distress. I directed her to my colleague next door for assistance.

Let your conscience be your guide in matters of what you offer students, but always be wary of offering anything medicinal.

> 6. A student walks in to your classroom complaining bitterly about the poor teaching ability of another teacher. This is not the first time you have heard complaints about this teacher. You also may not hold him or her in particular regard. The student then asks your opinion about this teacher.

So, ye who believe in truth at all times, how do you respond here? Do you agree with the student, allowing yourself to be known as the teacher who criticizes colleagues in front of students? Do you disagree with the student, thereby offering tacit approval of instructional competence that you do in fact find lacking? Do you say nothing?

Here you must tread with care. A student's disapproval of a teacher may be based on many factors, ranging from resentment about a single homework assignment to a long series of truly stulti-fying classes. At issue here is whether you believe you need to keep peace in the faculty lounge by keeping quiet when students complain about colleagues or whether you take it upon yourself to join your disapproval with theirs. What advantage do you gain by agreeing with them? What might you lose? Are you thinking value in discretion here? Quite so! However, compare that scenario to this one:

> 7. A student confides in you that another teacher has made inappropriate comments or has made the student feel uncomfortable by his or her actions, gestures, looks, or words.

This is altogether different. Sexual harassment policy established by schools mandates a response. Here you must advocate for the student, abide by the established policy, and speak with the immediate supervisor of the teacher involved.

A student once told me that a teacher made her feel uncomfortable by asking all the students to stand on their desks. As she was wearing a short skirt that day, the request made her feel funny, since she connected it with a vague feeling of unease she had long felt around this instructor. Was this harassment? Could this have been a misconstruction of an unusual classroom activity? It is not up to you to make such distinctions. The student feels unease, and you must report that unease to a supervisor. The supervisor is responsible for determining such distinctions and for mentoring (or, if appropriate, warning) the teacher in question. There will always be gradations in circumstances that could allow you to respond differently. The teacher must be savvy enough to recognize the proper response when those circumstances occur and be ready to make a decision, often in a matter of seconds.

> 8. You notice one of your students has his/her pants zipper undone.

You may think that teacher preparation is about readying yourself for the responsibility of bringing knowledge's light to a world darkened by ignorance, but I must tell you that in all my years of preparing teachers, the zipper question is the most common *what-if* question asked. What is it about zippers that make us all frenzied? What threat to universal order exists here?

Philosophy aside, the question persists. How do you draw the attention of such a student and avoid drawing other students' attention at the same time? Let's assume the solution is not to shout it out so everyone can hear or to whisper directly into the student's ear while the rest of the class is watching you and then the student's quick and embarrassed reaction.

Try a misdirection method instead. Direct the students' attention to the far side of the classroom while at the same time leaning over and whispering to the student in question. I warrant this will work with zippers undone or buttons undone or with visible snot or even with a fabric softener sheet poking out of a shirtsleeve (my own personal embarrassing moment). Crisis resolved, humiliation averted, the world can continue turning, and you can proceed with your mission.

> 9. A student expresses his or her love to you in a letter.

While you retain youth and energy, students will be drawn to that youthful energy. Some will translate that attraction into the crushes so common in school life. Face it, you are young, and some of your students will develop a crush on you. This unnerves the new teacher, and here one must respond with sensitivity and absolute clarity. Do not mince words, but do not belittle. Do not worry about hurtful feelings, and do not be anything but clear. Do not express thanks or appreciation for such words, for that may unintentionally encourage a student. Somewhere in your words there must be a clear message that says, "I am not here for that purpose for you."

In today's litigious society, you must be clear and forthright. You may experience deep feelings for your students, but the essential fact of the matter is that you are only a temporary presence in their lives, dedicated to assisting them to learn more and to feel better about themselves and their own worth and purpose in life. Then they will move on, and you will move on. You cannot be anything else to them. You cannot take them home, cannot keep them with you, cannot witness their progress through the stages of life, and cannot be a forever presence with them. Students may see you as a sounding board for their own attractiveness, and they may flirt innocently. You as teacher must recognize the ephemeral and unsubstantial nature of that flirtation and make no indication of acceptance or encouragement.

10. A student asks you to drive him or her home.

More situation challenges exist in the realm of the extracurricular than in the classroom. New teachers are expected to advise clubs, and in the club context, a teacher is more at ease with students, prompting circumstances that could blur the teacher-student distinction.

In this scenario different schools have different policies. Some schools may forbid transporting students in personal vehicles for safety reasons, while others may provide insurance riders that protect the teacher-driver under the policy of the school. You want the students to arrive home safely, but given the potential liability involved, you must be prudent. You want to avoid being in your car with one student, especially if that student is not of your gender. I advise against transporting students in your car altogether.

11. Two students begin to fight in your classroom.

This scenario is fraught with circumstantial elements. The age of the students and the volatility of their confrontation must be gauged. Your responsibility is for their safety, and you will have reflected before you begin work on what role you will play when a fight occurs. Even with that reflection, you may find yourself making a snap decision, and perhaps it will need to be different from the one you planned.

What has worked for me in fight situations is an understanding of fight protocol. Usually, one person is more aggressive or aggrieved than the other, who acts in a reactive rather than a proactive role. I probably would move quickly to the more aggressive of the two, thinking that the less aggressive combatant would be relieved about my interference and not try to sucker punch over my back. I would stand with legs apart and bottom of both palms against the attacker, repeating variations of "you don't want to do this." Maneuvering the more aggressive person toward the classroom door would be my path.

The circumstance of violence in schools usually occurs without warning, triggered by events in the "other discipline" of the school halls, the curriculum of who likes who; who betrayed whom; who thinks what of whom—the panoply of human aggression and hurt displayed so well in the halls where adolescents gather and move. It presents you with a real challenge. How will you respond? Will you yell out in an attempt to get help? Will you intervene? Will you flee? You really will not know until it occurs, and when you respond, you will respond based on your instincts. One thing is for sure, you will not respond based upon a careful reconsideration of this discussion or any other you may have had in your traditional teacher preparation courses. But you must and will respond, and in that response, you will learn something about yourself unrevealed in your professional preparation. But what about the moment you truly cannot foresee:

12. A student brandishes a weapon in your class.

Only once in my career did I disarm a student who brought a Bowie knife to class mainly to show off. I asked for it, he refused, dared me to take it from him. I did by using a simple and simply lucky gesture I learned in a martial arts class I took years before. But his stance was not threatening, nor his hold on the knife accurate enough to cause harm. I remanded him to the deans and trembled for the rest of the day.

I don't have an answer for this scenario. As I tell prospective teachers, my job is to protect students. Yet, I also want very much to live to walk my daughter down the aisle at her wedding, to watch my son grow to manhood, and to take my wife with me to my dotage. I frankly do not know if I would use my body to shield a student from harm or use a student to shield me from harm. You would think such thoughts would never need to surface in this line of work. But we all know today that the unthinkable does occur, and what we do under unthinkable circumstances remains a personal decision. Like police officers and fire fighters, teachers today may work in hazardous settings. It is our duty to protect as well as instruct their children.

But consider the complexity of protecting the children in your classroom. One of the prospective teachers I worked with was observing in an elementary class when the mother of one of the students entered the room. Enraged that her child had damaged a textbook and that the school had fined her, the mother ran to her child and began beating him. The teacher directed the other children to move away from the mother and her child but allowed her to continue to harm her child. At one point the child broke free and ran to huddle behind the legs of the student teacher, who stood frozen in fear. The mother finally dragged her child from the room.

What would you have done in this circumstance? Is your room a place where violence is never tolerated, where you will do whatever necessary to protect your children? What if that means preventing parents from doing what they may be doing at home? Or do you allow a parent the right to discipline a child, even if the other children witness an upsetting display of adult aggression? The situation happened just that fast, and the teacher responded instantly, albeit incorrectly in the eyes of the school district, which disciplined her for not intervening. The harrowing point is that the courses you are taking to prepare you to teach may not touch anywhere near this subject. They may, to use a metaphor I have used before, discuss John Dewey, but they will not prepare you to deal with Mrs. Dewey when she is beating up on Johnny in your classroom because she had to pay a fine.

This is why the late Dave Sanders of Columbine High School is a hero. Shot while directing students to a room away from his murderer, he acted as a human entrusted with the care of other humans. No one taught him what to do if someone began shooting at his students. No class in self-defense brought him any enlightenment. He acted as he would have had he been in any other profession. Sobering thoughts as you prepare to enter a world you and I hope will be full of papier-mâché, giggling, and easily resolved adolescent angst.

Expecting the Unexpected

Rushworth Kidder (1996) has written extensively and well on the situation ethics faced by teachers. His work at the Institute for Global

Ethics focuses on four major patterns that apply to nearly all unexpected situations that can occur in teaching:

1. Individual versus community, when the needs of the individual conflict with the needs of a group.

2. Truth versus honesty, when the integrity of an individual is at odds with that individual's responsibility.

3. Short-term versus long-term, when the needs of the moment clash with deferred needs.

4. Justice versus mercy, when fairness is in conflict with compassion.

Kidder's (1996) work on this subject merits close attention as you attempt to prepare for situations you cannot predict—the unexpected that requires immediate response. Here are scenarios prepared by my colleague and friend Dave Ripley for prospective teachers. How would you respond?

1. You are a high-school women's basketball coach and one of your athletes tells you her stepfather has been physically abusing her. She begs you not to tell anyone as she is afraid that the stepfather will harm her mother or her younger sister.

2. You are a middle-school teacher and a parent calls you, claiming that you called her son "stupid." What you did say, after the boy made an inappropriate comment in class, was that his point "was the stupidest thing you ever heard." You deny calling the boy "stupid" but sense that the parent will contact the principal if you do not apologize.

3. You are a new teacher in an upper middle-class suburban high school district. Several students ask your help in approaching the administration seeking permission to form a gay/lesbian student organization, which they would like you to sponsor.

4. You are a second-grade teacher and one of your students, an especially needy and insecure lad, has gotten into the habit of giving you a hug at the end of every day. A veteran teacher enters the room while this is taking place, seems surprised, but says nothing.

5. A fifth-grade student in your class has a learning disability in reading. She benefits greatly from taking her tests and quizzes with

the resource teacher, who can read questions aloud and clarify terms, but the girl hates being "singled out" when she leaves the room. You could probably support her more in class to her benefit but at the expense of time and attention to your other students.

6. You are a high-school coach having a successful season. The team has begun going out for pizza after each contest, and they are eager to invite you. You note during conversations that the students have begun to regard you as one of the group. You enjoy the fellowship of these students but worry about blurring the lines between teacher and student.

Fascinating. The situation ethics of teaching approaches the complexity of chess and bridge—endless combinations of circumstances and participants that require you to make decisions, important decisions, that will in part define your success as a teacher. But traditional professional preparation programs pay scant attention to this subject.

When I first began appearing as a guest speaker in university methodology classes, I was thunderstruck by the unending desire of prospective teachers for answers to *what-if* questions. The gulf between the theoretician and the practitioner could not be wider than in this area, and the savvy new teacher will learn to acquire a support group and a mentor for help in considering these circumstances.

Sometimes the interaction of humans provides moments no educator could ever predict. One summer, I was hired as a tutor for a young man recovering from major surgery. We developed a rapport that continued as the fall began, and he was assigned to my class. One day as he entered the classroom wearing a jacket, I noticed a piece of a plastic bag sticking out of his pocket. "Hey," I shouted to all present, "what have we here, your drug stash?" and I tugged at the plastic, suddenly producing a rather large bag filled with reefers. The moment froze like a scene in a Brueghel painting. The kids looked at me, the kid looked at me, I looked at the bag—the moment froze in time. Did I just do an illegal search and seizure? Could I keep the bag? Return the bag in a room full of witnesses? Help! Yikes! As it turned out, I confiscated the bag and reported the incident to the deans, receiving a modest rebuke for searching a student.

At the time, search and seizure laws on school grounds were vague. Currently, schools have the authority to conduct locker searches for contraband, though the extent of personal searches requires careful consideration, far more consideration than my action offered. While school lockers have been deemed to be not the sole property of students (*Zamora v Pomeroy,* 639F 2d, 665), students must be given notice that their right to privacy is limited. The case of *State of New Jersey v Moore* (1992) allows searches of book bags, pockets, or purses, but the reason for the search must be expressed and the search must end if it reveals no prohibited items. *The National Association of Attorneys General School Search Reference Guide of 1999* states that "the right of freedom of movement enjoyed by school age children is far more limited than the right of liberty enjoyed by adult citizens. . . . Schools may impose significant restrictions . . . also on their ability to use and possess personal property." The U.S. Supreme Court in the case of *New Jersey v T.L.O.* recognized that "the preservation of order and of a proper educational environment requires close supervision of children." This circumstance surfaces frequently in U.S. classrooms, requiring judicial oversight. "The U.S. Supreme Court is set to hear the case of a young Arizona honor student who was strip-searched in the eighth grade by school officials looking for ibuprofen pills." (http://www.cbsnews.com/stories/2009/04/20/earlyshow/ main4956242.shtml)

The net result of these decisions is that while students do possess the rights to privacy of person as guaranteed by the Fourth Amendment to the U.S. Constitution, those rights are balanced by a school's responsibility to protect its students. Therefore school officials and teachers can conduct searches when they have a reason to suspect a school law has been or will be violated, or if students are in danger. The law even specifies when searches are in order.

About this time you may be wondering why this discussion is so far afield from field trips and jack-o'-lanterns on bulletin boards and apples on the big desk. Teaching situations are so varied and compelling in their complexity! Your response to scenarios you never thought you would encounter will be more indicative of your effect than the grades you earned in your education courses.

PRACTICING FOR "WHAT IF"

My colleague Peg Cain approaches the subject of situation ethics in teaching with a set of cards dispensed in her classes with prospective teachers. You too can practice the *what-if* game and seek advice from veteran teachers, even if only to provide a plan of action in considering your own responses to what can occur in the amazing dynamic that is the American classroom.

What will you do when

- A student calls you by your first name?
- A student asks if you have ever taken hallucinogens?
- A parent says you don't have enough experience to teach?
- A student tells you "My mother is dying"?
- A sixth-grader tells you she's pregnant?
- A parent comes on to you?
- A colleague details your mistakes at the faculty lunch table?
- You notice a student crying in class?
- A student says, "We learned this last year"?
- A student says, "I'm dropping out as soon as I'm sixteen"?
- A student calls another a "faggot"?
- A student says to you, "Fuck you"?
- A student says to you, "My mother's a slut"?
- A student throws up?
- A bee enters the classroom?
- You feel an attraction to a student?
- A student farts?
- A student becomes the class victim?
- A student says, "I was never good in [the subject you teach]"?
- A student consistently smells bad?
- A student faints?
- You don't know the answer to a question?
- A student asks, "Are you a virgin"?
- A student says, "This is so stupid!"?
- A student says, "I hate this school"?
- A student asks, "When are we ever going to use this stuff in real life"?
- A student says, "I turned my paper in—you must have lost it"?
- A student reports another student is cheating?
- A student plagiarizes?
- A student says, "You're boring"?
- A student says, "My dad says teachers are lazy because they only work 180 days a year"?
- You see a weapon in someone's locker?

- There's a mouse in the classroom?
- A student asks, "Are you living with your boyfriend/girlfriend"?
- A student reports one of her classmates is sexually involved with a teacher?
- You lose your grade book?
- A student gives you an expensive Christmas present?
- Money is missing from your desk?
- You catch a boy and a girl, or two boys or two girls, half-naked in the janitor's closet?
- A girl wears provocative clothing in the classroom, causing disruption?
- A boy enters wearing a T-shirt with words on it you find offensive?
- A student performs well on in-class assignments but never turns in homework?
- A student is regularly absent on test day?
- A student tells you she or he must take medication periodically throughout the day?
- A student says, "I can't take this test. I have PMS"?
- A student says, "This is my favorite class"?
- A student looks at another student's paper during a test?
- Your students will not follow directions?
- Your students wander the room at will?
- You cannot fight the urge to be angry or to cry?

More than a parlor game, these exercises will bring you to a critical understanding that your stature as a teacher will derive from more than the subject matter that you have learned to teach. You cannot underestimate the need for subject matter mastery, but there also is this other situational element of the profession that requires your quick and accurate decision. Let your tenets be your guide.

REFLECTIVE EXERCISE

Try to determine how you would respond to any of the fifty situations presented here. Compare yours to a colleague's decision. Then find a veteran teacher and compare both responses to the veteran's. Shouldn't there be an encyclopedia of these somewhere? Start crafting yours.

CHAPTER FIFTEEN

Major Stresses in the Teaching Profession

The Balancing Act

[The Teaching Life and Having a Life]

W e teachers are great at complaining, great at recognizing the gulf of difference in our work lives as opposed to our friends outside of teaching. The first thing noticed when the group of friends graduate college, find their initial jobs, and settle into them is the great difference in the teacher's life in comparison to other workers' lives. The salesperson and the analyst and the bricklayer and the stock broker and the shopkeeper and the buyer walk away at work day's end from their job responsibilities. They gather at the pub on weekends or weekdays and note the teacher's absence or preoccupation. The teacher's job, you see, is always there. To teach is to work and live in a perpetual state of imbalance. Homework waits. The planning must be done. The reflection on the day's circumstances must be taken. How did it go wrong today? What must be done differently? Why is this one sad, that one preoccupied? How can I get my principal to see my worth? Do I have worth? What if I tried this technique, or took them there? Add to these thoughts the requirements of spouse or significant other, family and children, graduate class and hobby, and you have the perpetual balancing act that is the teacher's life. There are so few occupations that dominate life so much. Postal workers come close, because their work never truly is finished, and we laugh along with Newman in *Seinfeld* when he snarls, "It's always there!" My wife's work in IT human relations systems has brought her sixty-hour work weeks and the constant pressure to produce and keep pace with deadlines. But it is an easier act of compensating when you've had over twenty years experience than it is when you've had twenty weeks worth. In teaching, *they* are always there—your students and their needs and problems, and your challenges with them—in the room, to and from work, preparing for the next day, as you wrestle some moments to yourself, while staring at the ceiling waiting for sleep.

For the new teacher, this life discipline overwhelms and can be the source of error and frustration. It contributes to why so many leave the profession, added with the difficulty obtaining respect and the varying capabilities of administrators to help. How does one combat the predominance teaching can have on your life?

You should practice strengthening your resiliency by knowing yourself well enough to apply counterbalance when you lean too far in one direction—either moroseness or overextension on work requirements. All jobs and all personal relationships have their disappointments and frustrations. Knowing temporary downs from serious moments will keep you on a more even keel.

Your intuitive nature will activate when you are in the company of burned-out teachers. They have visible signs and sounds that emanate defeat, exhaustion, and hopelessness. You know they did not start out in the profession that way, but a series of who knows what events, both personal and professional, have led them down a spiral into cynical immobility. They should leave, but can't. They don't care anymore but must pretend to do so. Every administrative step is criticized, every slight magnified to grievance level diatribe. Good Lord, are these people sad and deadening to be around! Look at them carefully and see yourself taking their place if you don't focus on maintaining the balancing act that will keep you active and viable. I often advise new teachers to study negative teaching traits in the belief that learning by negation is as valuable as learning by modeling. You cannot change the low morale in someone as easily as you can be infected by it—so don't get too close to the radioactive negativity of the burned-out teacher—just enough to smell and see the warning signs so you can sense the signs on you.

Why You Must Remain a Teacher

This chapter addresses frustration, not the kind engendered by your efforts or your students' but by the nature of the teaching profession and by some of those within it. If you are reading this book, then you are striving to become an excellent teacher. You fear that the nation has too many teachers who do not strive for excellence and you have vowed you will not be one of them. You will put in hours untold perfecting your craft. Your personal life will be affected by your dedication. You will learn from your mistakes. But along the way you will also learn that there are some truths inherent in our profession that will infuriate you. This chapter focuses on two of those major stressors:

- The absence of a career ladder in our profession's definition of a teacher.
- The presence in our profession of colleagues who cannot or will not work to improve their craft, thereby degrading the title "teacher."

I focus on these aspects because as you acclimate to teaching during years two through five and begin to enlarge your view of our profession, these stressors will frustrate you.

You may be tempted to speak out, but you will also perceive that the teaching profession, like many others, has its own code of silence. You may be tempted to move toward an activist role in improving the standards of our profession, but you will also definitely feel the conformist's pull. A great number of teachers leave the profession after five years, and I hope you will be able to resist that trend. Perhaps this chapter can help you anticipate and withstand some of the major disappointments you will encounter as you move toward excellence in teaching.

The Teacher-Hero

Study the teacher-heroes you meet on your journey toward excellence. Here are some of the characteristics you will notice:

Excellent teachers study their own students. The first thing you may notice when observing a teacher-hero with children is her absolute refusal to give up on a student, ever. Patient and resourceful, she resonates with the idea that you cannot be a teacher unless you are a student of your students. She finds what appeals to that most reluctant student and uses it to bring that child ever closer to loving knowledge.

Excellent teachers want to do more. His advocacy for his students prompts him to use his own money or the good nature of those he knows to acquire the resources his students need. He constantly works at his craft, wondering what more he can do when he does so much already. The students sense this. The parents bless him for it. Still he frets about what more he can do.

Excellent teachers make careful choices. She may be beloved as a teacher, but she does not require love in order to help her students achieve. The most ornery and unlovable student is as vital to her as the most fawning one. She strives to show every student how learning is connected to life. She is relentless in finding reason to praise. She knows her daily choices and decisions carry a consequence of either life with purpose or dreary emptiness for her students. She chooses wisely.

Excellent teachers respect their profession and their colleagues. He takes risks, even though missed opportunities and errors trouble his conscience. His passion for achievement may at times isolate him from his colleagues, but he will reach out for support and to offer comfort to those in his profession who care as deeply as he does. Together, they can withstand the inanity and the misery and the anguish and the bureaucracy in teaching to achieve a triumph for the children.

Most telling of all attributes, the teacher-hero shuns the title and shies away from accolades. Drawing attention to her own unique talents as teacher shifts the focus away from students, and for the excellent teacher, the children and only the children matter.

PROBLEM: LIMITED PROFESSIONAL PROGRESSION

Teacher-heroes are legendary and numerous. Ask the children, and without guile or agenda they will point them out to you. Ask the administrator or the colleague unsullied by jealousy, and they will name them. And in the *should-be* world, such teacher-heroes would enjoy the same rewards given to those who are deeply talented in the business world: salary bonuses, opportunities to share their leadership theories with younger colleagues, and important stakes in the decision-making process of the building.

But in the *can't-be* world the teacher-hero inhabits, there are no preferred parking spots. The teacher-hero will earn what everyone else earns who has her years in the profession and her kind of degree. He will teach the same hours and the same number of courses as a first-year teacher, and he will endure the same inane study hall assignments. If his ambition warrants it, he will progress in the only way we have devised for career progress in American education: to administration, away from children and away from the very substance that brought him to teaching excellence in the first place.

We must devise new and different ways to reward our teacher-heroes. The teacher-hero is not an inexhaustible resource. In a society that recognizes merit with money, and a system chary of offering extra compensation to the excellent teacher, how can such talent be found, nurtured, and retained?

National Board Certification

One possibility for a better form of teacher compensation comes from the National Board for Professional Teaching Standards, which has developed and identified five core attributes of accomplished teaching and the means by which those attributes can be evidenced. The process is rigorous, proven, and national in scope, and some courageous states award a salary adjustment to teachers who achieve national board certification.

Pay Equity

But we should go further than providing salary enhancement to the teacher-hero for achieving National Board certification. The whole traditional structure of teacher compensation based on years of experience and acquisition of collegiate units has become a disservice to teachers. We are all on a continuum of acquired skills. The emerging teacher has different challenges and successes than the veteran teacher does, and it is ludicrous to expect a twenty-two-year-old novice teacher to command the same knowledge base as a twenty-two-year veteran teacher. The teacher's knowledge base grows with time and practice, and teachers should be recompensed when they demonstrate observable improvements in teaching skills, classroom practice, and achieving educational goals.

The private sector has developed new compensation structures based on skills and expertise, goal accomplishment by individuals and by groups. Those deeply concerned about teaching—practitioners and theoreticians, union leaders, rank and file teachers, business leaders, parents—must come together to agree to a necessary task: revamping the teacher compensation system. How many brilliant people do you think we can continue to attract to the teaching profession when there are schools with dilapidated facilities, insufficient resources, limited self-determination, and abysmal compensation? Equity in educational funding is an issue that needs discussion as well, but our immediate need is to attract the truly talented and pay them as well as other professions of great talent for doing the most vital work ever devised—teaching children.

PROBLEM: THE CYNICAL COLLEAGUE

"They pay me whether they learn or not" and "Why are you doing so much? You're making us look bad by comparison." In my years of working with prospective teachers, hearing those words is the single greatest disappointment they express after entering the profession. Colleagues who do not care, are not motivated, go through the motions, offer disservice to children with their cynicism and their distrust—such colleagues will criticize the novice teacher for having energy and positivism. They will warn the new teacher of disappointments to come. Their infectious brand of "who-do-you-think-you-are?" is an age-old shield to divert light from their ineptitude. Such teachers will absolutely sap your strength if you allow them to do so.

The majority of the people you meet on your teaching journey will be good, honest, decent, and effective. Many will offer you their ideas and their resources. Some will become your friends for life. But be wary of those in our profession who taint its name. They demoralize both practitioner and child. And, maddeningly, the profession does not have swift mechanisms to deal with them.

Example: On the first day of my tenth year of teaching, our superintendent, an always charming man who dressed in suits the color of autumnal wheat, gathered all the teachers in my district to explain the newest evaluation system the district would employ: "It is just a matter of logic that one of you in here is the worst teacher in the district." Was this comment intended to inform? . . . assist? . . . stigmatize? That was never quite explained to us. Huffy and indignant, we moved off to open our classroom windows and work out that rancid smell each summer layered on the walls, fully believing we were not the worst teachers in the district.

What is more infuriating is that, short of recognizing criminality, any evaluation system, new or not, cannot compel the negative teacher to improve nor threaten that teacher with removal from the profession. There in your midst such teachers will remain, neither inspiring nor struggling to improve nor reflecting on their practice, not really doing anything save serving as an indictment to your diligence. And these representatives of sloth and ignorance who work alongside the industry and excellence of teacher-heroes are paid the same and have exactly the same responsibilities.

Why You Must Remain a Teacher

While you are working and worrying and improving and reflecting, you may get the distinct and unnerving sense that those in your profession who are cynical may be harming scores or hundreds of children yearly. While you become ever more mindful of the damage that can be done by the teaching profession at its worst, you will also be asking yourself who will protect the children? That is why you must remain and persevere.

When You Must Stop Being a Teacher

You may not choose to voice your distaste for your cynical colleagues, and you can leave the room when you hear them blaming parents, society, or anything but themselves for their own failures, but you must hang on until or unless you yourself feel a pull away from the energies that brought you to teaching. If you start to see hopelessness instead of potential in your students' faces, if you start to feel drawn to the anger and negativity of your colleagues, you may have become infected with a cynicism you absolutely cannot hide from your students. They will see it, they will use it to measure their own tentative sense of worth, and they will confirm your prediction that they cannot succeed. If you sense that change, find something else to do with your life. The world is wide and the economy varied, offering you many avenues that can reward and suffice.

How You Can Keep Hope Alive

But if you resent such negativity, if you carry in you some sense of energy and belief in the power of the motivated mind to learn, if you believe that short of pathology your students can learn, then for their sake you must remain. Your stature as a teacher will grow and your development as a hero will continue. You may even wish to broaden your effect within the school community. I hope soon there is a day when your effort and your success will result in an evolution of your role as teacher. Hope drives the excellent teacher onward. Keep it alive in yourself and in the children you encounter. Be part of those who will make the *will-be* world for this profession.

REFLECTIVE EXERCISES

• *Study the ineffective teacher.* When you come across a teacher who the children have rejected or about whom colleagues have commented, examine his methods. Listen to him talk about children during lunch. Is there more cynicism than optimism in his words? Learn what not to do and what not to believe from this teacher's example.

• Imagine being able to work with children, lead the school, and make decisions that positively impact the educational experience. Could you help younger teachers acquire your sense of mission? Can you imagine an educational community with the flexibility to allow you to develop into a leader on a par with those in the business community?

Task for reflection: Upon whom can you rely? Who can you count on for support?

CHAPTER SIXTEEN

The Paperwork Can Kill You

Thoughts on Technology

In my vision of the almost perfect school, the key to teacher effectiveness would be every four teachers sharing an administrative assistant. In the business world, success is achieved through delegation. Not only is delegation good for business organization, it also ensures mental stability! Only in the teaching world does one find a profession so insistent that everyone manage his or her own paperwork and handle every detail personally. Until you have entered this profession, you will not truly realize the immensity of the paperwork demands upon you or how command of that paperwork will define your effectiveness to your administrators. Here is a cruel truism: You can work with intensive concentration on improving your lesson plans, but if you keep sloppy grade books and attendance records you will seal your doom. You may have all your students excited about learning, but if you forget to send home notes to parents about immunization, then you will have a cross principal appearing at your classroom door. You must devise a method of handling paperwork that will allow you to work on the most essential part of your job. I recommend triage, a term from medical practice, in which you sort by priority the paperwork that appears in your mailbox and deal with it in order of its importance.

GRADE BOOKS AND ATTENDANCE RECORDS

There are really only two parts of school paperwork you must place at absolute top priority: assigning grades in your grade book and keeping up-to-date attendance records. Both grade books and attendance records are legal documents that testify to the work you have done with your students, signified by a record of their academic progress, and a record of their daily presence or absence.

In my work with prospective teachers, I have found that inadequate work with the grade book and attendance keeping are the most serious threats to their continuing in the profession. You must assign work and that work must be adjudged and returned and recorded. You must show you know who is in front of you each day, and some schools may insist that you use arcane symbols to signify variations in a student's presence or absence: excused or unexcused, field trip absence, suspension, ill during class, parent picking up. In these matters, modeling can be a lifesaver. Copy your mentor's approach if you have been assigned a mentor. If not, then ask the students who is the best teacher in the building and befriend that teacher as a mentor.

STUDENT INFORMATION AND PARENT MESSAGES

After you have acquired a system you are comfortable with for grade books and attendance records, then move on to material about specific students (medical information, field trip forms, and so forth), followed by phone messages from parents.

These are the top four holy grails of teacher paperwork. No administrator will stand for sloppiness in grade books or attendance records. Colleagues who request information from you about your students will be miffed and spread that disdain to others if you do not reply to a counselor's request for information or homework assignments for absent students. No parent will stand for your not returning a phone message.

Almost everything else not directly relating to your students can be triaged until later. I used to gather all the "later" mail into a box to look at once a week. Of course, everyone who sends you paper believes it essential. But you have only four essentials:

1. Grade books

2. Attendance records

3. Information about specific students

4. Phone messages from parents

Everything else can wait.

The Important Role of Technology in Your Teaching

The more technologically savvy a teacher becomes, the more he or she becomes open-minded about integrating technology into classroom practice, the faster that teacher improves. Currently we have a digital divide not only between resource-rich and resource-poor schools, but between teachers who shun, fear, or belittle technology and a growing student populace for which technology is second nature, virtually their sole source for reading, entertainment, communication, and social interaction. To not utilize a modality students find central to their lives and use with ease as a conduit to classroom learning places stress on a teacher's ability to reach students. Once upon a time it was considered quaint and conservative to claim Luddite-like ignorance of technology in school use. Now that stance is just seen as teacher camouflage for the inability or unwillingness to learn how best to reach students.

At the very least, the plethora of grade book technologies available today allows teachers to give students and their parents or guardians anytime access to student academic progress. It demystifies the process of learning and increases partnering with parents. Teachers who launch Web sites open their classroom doors wider to allow a learning community of children and parents to develop, increasing communication possibilities with busy parents, and helping students engage in technology to increase their learning potential.

So at the very least, use of technology allows teachers to improve their assessment tools and communication opportunities with students and their parents.

But of course there is so much more that teachers can do using technology. Kelly, McCain, and Jukes, in their work *Teaching the Digital Generation* (2009) offer superb advice in this area. Their major thesis is compelling—students brought up in digital technology now learn in a totally different way. Today's teachers who do not embrace and use technology consign their students to irrelevant learning. With high-school dropouts numbering well over one million nationwide annually, their call is for a new world order in high-school design. The authors believe high schools have wallowed in mediocrity and irrelevance and need total redesign to provide more choice in order to have students with more agility than scoring well on standardized tests. High schools of the industrial age, based on mass production techniques paralleling the assembly line with an eye on the agrarian needs of a bygone America, only hurt students. The authors' indictment could not be clearer: Because we of an older generation grew up without technology as a central focus of our lives, and our teachers were even less technologically exposed, we have difficulty seeing how technology can transform both teaching and learning. At best, we half-heartedly try through using an overhead projector or Scan-Tron tests to believe we are truly incorporating technology. We delude. We think technology is not needed. We could not be more wrong. "Due to the combination of their non-digital upbringing and their exposure to the traditional ideas of what teaching looks like, adult educators have a great deal of difficulty seeing how technology could significantly change the way teaching, learning, and assessment happens. They bring an outdated twentieth century perspective to the way they use technology for learning that views technology as a nonessential add-on to the teaching process. As a result, technology use is at best supplemental to the teaching given by the teacher, at worse, not needed at all (Jakes et al., 233).

Remember also that there abound in this country schools with woeful technology, and many students do not have access to the digital wonderland. In striving to provide equal access to all students, equal access to excellent instruction is also a goal to attain and that excellence encompasses more than technological wherewithal. Just observe a great teacher and that teacher's technique transcends many circumstances and obstacles.

Great help abounds online for those catching up on the digital wave. Two Web sites of note, www.education-world.com and www.audio-ed-online.com, offer multiples of examples and links to help new teachers with integration. School districts are becoming more aware of the advantages in technology by recommending and incorporating laptop, iPod, podcasts and interactive games into the school experience. The Mind Institute of California, www.mindinst.org, has created superb products for improving student abilities in mathematics using game technology and music.

There was a common tale told in the Chicago area about certain schools rushing to acquire technology and then that technology remained under lock and key or still in original packaging because of the absence of professional development to improve teacher ability and knowledge of its use. We have offered our profession a disservice by remaining technologically stunted, allowing a tool so well-used and understood by students to go unused. In poorer communities, acccss alone further stunts the educational development of students, who have little or no access to computer technology in school or at home.

These lapses should serve as a spur to action for you as prospective or new teachers to learn all you can about integrating technology into your teaching, assessment, and diagnostic skill set.

If I could offer one minute example, it would be my first-hand knowledge of the advantage of using YouTube in my recent teaching. While frequently referencing works of art, music, film, or poetry in my units, I have found it a great dimension-adder to my work by having that instantaneous access and demonstration. In one class, we were talking about the nature of free will and fate, and the interaction between. The conversation steered toward the futuristic movie *Minority Report* in which law enforcement in the future is aided by preternatural knowledge in the form of three empaths of when a crime was going to be committed in the future, allowing intervention (and arrest) of persons engaging in "pre-crime." While my meager words do not give this interesting premise justice, our conversation moved to a particular scene in the movie, and in six seconds through accessing YouTube, I found that scene, vivifying in my students' minds the point at the point of discussion. Besides being immediate, it was just totally cool. Discussion of ska as a musical derivation of reggae allowed me to show examples of The Mighty Mighty Bosstones treatment of it in their '80s song "The Impression That

I Get." The world is opened wide with just this simplistic use. Your work will use it to far more dimension and impact.

Think about this as a goal—five years from the start of your career, be at a point where you would be at a distinct disadvantage in your teaching if all the technology you use would be taken away. This from someone who once believed the best technology there could be was a well-constructed book and a room with adequate temperature and lighting. The classroom and its teacher must evolve into something far beyond twenty-first century, and our teachers must lead the charge rather than defer its inclusion or deny its existence.

Reflective Exercise

Triage your mail. Spend a few weeks separating the essential from the superfluous in your home mailbox. Pay a few bills on time and answer a few letters from friends. Then review your home-mail method template to duplicate or improve for your professional mail.

Also, plan to add as much knowledge about technology into your work as you can in the first five years of your career or else be always behind an important curve.

CHAPTER SEVENTEEN

Living in Testmania

Staying True to Your Core

T he pressure to reduce all learning into test performance and all teaching to test preparation has never been stronger. The education and funding community all hail test performance as the key to proof of effectiveness. My years of teaching brought me to the beginning of this trend, when state tests were introduced with the codicil that they would never be used for evaluating teacher effectiveness. Posh! The decade of the '80s brought us the Great Perception foisted on our profession by the powerful: Teachers are the problem, they cannot be trusted, and we must use objective measurements of what students know to judge what teachers do. Cottage industries in test preparation and delivery sprang like wildcat oil companies. There was money to be made in doubting teachers and in requiring that all (students, of course, but others argued for teachers too) take tests. The intrusion of test preparation and test days starting in a few grades were expanded in the Bush years until one day we will be testing every child at every grade every so often often enough to give schooling the image of perpetual test taking. Lesson plans become tangents to test questions anticipated. Teaching has become a profession where nobility and passion lose out to formula and rote. Test anxiety in children will become the new target with cottage industries of test preparation (and, just watch, pharma-copoeia!) springing up to offer succor.

This constant pressure has brought about some interesting consequences. Students in highly challenging high-school settings are

more and more delaying the start of college for travel and volun-
teerism. Antianxiety medications are prolific in our society as is
teenage depression. We have taken the idle threat of the permanent
record and turned it into a twenty-first century all-out assault on
teaching to or for anything but the test.

With your first assignment, you will gauge the degree of
Testmania in your school. New and anxious to please, with an already
deep sense of insecurity about your ability, the temptation will be
strong to dive in deep to the test-preparation approach to teaching. It
will seem so easy—there are the types of questions that will be asked
on some test day, and there are the workbooks and lesson plans that
make the class hour seem to fly by. You can do whole units on analogies, whole segments of lessons on types of writing. You could create
a classroom Potemkin village of preparation without a core, without
a clue if you follow the test-maker's guides and the teacher-proof
curriculum.

You will thereby sell your soul, sell your students short, and sell
out the proud profession you have joined.

You must resist! But as any true member of the resistance, you
must do so cleverly. You must take the core of your tenets, the
reasons why you teach the lessons you wish to impart, and embed
test-making tools within them. *Instead of teaching to the test, you
teach to your tenets, and the correlation to success in test taking will
be made thereby.* You don't ever give up the soul of your teaching—
but first you must have a soul of your teaching identified!

The damnable thing about life in Testmania is that it always
seems the substance of tests seems to evade the lessons you teach. If
analogies were the standard by which logical reasoning is known,
why did we not spend hours and weeks on analogies? The test mak-
ers like test situations like analogies because they can be quickly
graded. How many thoughtful decisions do you want your students
to make within seconds unless life or liberty is at stake? To the
casual cynic, it would appear as if what we were taught was irrelevant in the analogy world. But how many weeks do we devote to the
comma—that spurious moment of pause in our thought flow. In
Testmania, it seems that comma knowledge is the most superior
form of language perception. Then should we teach comma, comma,
comma, until the very heart and juice of language is wrung dry? The
value in Testmania does not match the value in becoming productive
citizens. It is reductive, narrow learning at its least dimensional. It

will bring out students noting the pause in the sentence, "Oh, look out, a boulder descends above us," long enough for the boulder to descend!

A recent study by the Consortium on Chicago School Research at the University of Chicago (2008) has proved a most interesting counterpoint to helping students cram for tests like the ACT (the test of choice for high-school juniors and seniors in the Midwest). Demand for accountability and progress has infused the high-school upper class years' experience with test taking preparation, which eats into class time, and to what end? The study showed "the more that schools emphasize test preparation in class, the lower are their students' ACT scores" (Allensworth, 2008, 25). The very fact that the nature of the ACT is "designed not to be influenced by test preparation and strategies" (Allenworth, 2008, 24) should inform educators that more time must be taken to develop the kind of thinking that college courses require. Allensworth (2008) states "the broad content coverage that is typical in high school classes is not sufficient preparation for the ACT or for the demands of college course work. The low scores that students receive on the ACT indicate that students are not sufficiently learning these analytic schools while in high school" (2).

There are those who argue that tests such as the ACT contain embedded bias, and the Allensworth (2008) report concedes such concern: "Among students with a GPA of 3.5 or higher, African American students scored, on average, five points below white students, and Latino students scored three to four points below white students. . . . This is a disturbing pattern and may suggest possible racial bias in scores" (18). The reason achievement gap may exist according to the study has more to say about the access to quality instruction: "The main reason there are large racial/ethnic gaps in eleventh-grade ACT scores among Chicago Public Schools students with similar GPAs is that there are large racial/ethnic gaps in skill levels when students enter high school. . . . Many Latino and African American students are working hard and earning A's in their classes, but because they started so far behind their white and Asian peers in academic skills, their ACT scores remain several points lower. . . . Large racial gaps in academic preparation prior to high school are a major concern" (Allensworth, 2008, 25–26).

In haste to make up for less than stout academic preparation, high schools try to fill the students with test-taking strategies that (so say the cottage industries) promise to make up for the dearth in academic preparation provided to such students. But the during class or evening class, preparation does little but mask the true shame and blame on those in our profession who do not stretch student abilities, who shy away from setting the bar high for them as a camouflage for their own instructional inadequacies. Worse of all, such manic approach to test preparation, and the inevitable stress it places on our students, masks our inability to present to those students who most need and deserve the very best in instructional ability.

Again I use the analogy to musicians. If they think where to put their fingers and when to breathe and move, their art is lost. They place the where-to-put-their-fingers and when-to-breathe-and-move lessons *in the context of a greater thing, not in place of the greater thing!* Testmania makes the lesser thing the only thing, and it must be artfully resisted and redirected.

This is not to damn all forms of assessment. How else will you know if what you are doing is working? The purest and most important reason for assessing your students is to inform your instruction and to provide feedback to your students. Your professional growth and the growth of your students are key. Done as a spurious hope of assuaging administrator concerns about your state report card, ultimately runs counter to your aim.

REFLECTIVE EXERCISE

Task: Look at any test-taking concept that will appear on any test and see how you can approach that concept in a roundabout and deeper way using the substance of your tenets expanded to lesson or discussion.

Epilogue

Group Hug

After the riots in Chicago during the 1968 Democratic National Convention, the Daley administration put out a documentary defending their actions entitled "What Trees Do They Plant?" While the film itself may have created varied opinions, its title always stuck with me as a benchmark in determining whether I or those I meet have done well with the legacy bequeathed to us.

When I was a young man and would complain about something, my father would say, "And do your arms move? Your brain, it works pretty good? Can your legs walk you to a better situation?" When I was a young teacher listening to the complaints of high school students, I would smile and nod sympathetically, then plan a future field trip to the Shriner's Hospital for Crippled Children in Chicago. One year, after watching the staff work with those wonderful children and then listening to my students' quiet sniffling on the way back, one student looked up at me and said, "We haven't done anything with our lives."

"Not yet," I responded, "but there's still time."

I hold a great respect for the tree planters I have met in my life. The desire to find purpose in life by helping others find purpose in theirs is a blessed way to live. I have met people who commanded six-figure salaries who were totally unhappy with what they have contributed to life and more than willing to move to a job that pays a fraction of what they earned, one that provides all the frustration and challenge one can tolerate: public school teaching. And they are loving it. It is more than mere missionary zeal and more than mere masochism.

Done well, teaching is immensely rewarding. If you are deeply within it, keep a-going. If you are preparing to enter, hurry up and get in here. Children need you! If your heart is pure and your mind intent, the trees you plant will blossom.

WALKING OUT TO YOUR
FIRST DAY, YEAR, CAREER

You know you probably experienced a few hundred million words from your professors or the textbooks you encountered through teacher preparation, and you should have encountered a few hundred million pragmatic more. I hope that these few tens of thousands you've been kind enough to wade through have helped some. But the truth of it all is you can have the Oxford English Dictionary of Teaching Circumstances: situations, methodology and whaddya-do-when's in front of you, and it still will not be enough. The U.S. teaching journey has attracted millions of Americans, been abandoned by millions, encountered by millions, and it remains a singular journey. Help abounds, help as near as next door and your keyboard, your kindly professor, friends, and significant others. Heck, even I'd write back if you e-mailed me. But you are the sole adult that must enter the experience alone. For in your classroom, the most amazing, terrifying, emotional, boring, mundane, and occasionally transformative moments can happen. You can also metaphorically fall flat on your face, discover how little you really know about subject, about kids, about yourself, about the hierarchy, and iconography of schools. You have joined a profession that has to fight to be considered a profession, attacked by all sides, even within your community, distrusted, ridiculed. You have to think hard to think of examples of other professions so maligned. Doctors are replete on television shows, and they are written about romantically. The young interns love each other, the more experienced show them the way, then everyone seems to drink through the evening and couple. Lawyers are written as devious and dubious and within their ranks brave ones rise to champion the right and argue with passion. Then they drink through the evenings and couple. Cops are depicted as clannish and edgy, fighting valiantly to keep the dark sides of society they see daily from seeping into their personal lives, and in the evening they, well, you get the picture—though shows about cops show more misogyny, failed marriages, and boorish behavior than lawyer and doctor shows, mostly because the bulk of the casts are young, searching, unsure. Well, you begin the teacher journey as young, searching, and unsure as well. Given the preponderance of shows of the other three professions, teacher shows are rare, brief in their duration, and inaccurate. Ever notice in television shows about teachers the very act of good teaching is never shown? The doctors get to get it right, and the lawyers make their summations and oftentimes win cases, but think about a true successful moment of teaching depicted on film—and your list will be small. There are plenty of hilarious, insulting, and otherwise inaccurate moments. But outside of *Stand and Deliver,* your look for a true teaching model will have to come from within or those who inspired you to take this path.

Invariably, when I end sessions with prospective teachers, they're saying their goodbyes and gathering their things, and I'm saying, "Wait! There's more I have to tell you. Hold on, just one more thing." Perhaps I'm endured like Polonius, the parent who has twenty pieces of advice to a rolling-eyed child, but discussion about this profession and how best to do it can be endless. There really can be no one compendium of "when this happens—do this" knowledge that will allow the start of your teaching career to be worry and error-free. I remember my poetry professor's phrase from Paul Valéry: "A poem is never finished. It is abandoned." I know there are topics I've yet to expand upon for you: assessment practices, altering your assignments for the differing learning styles of your students, cueing in on resources for grants (of which I am aware in the Chicago area but numb and dumb outside). Plenty of people smarter and more research-oriented than I have great advice for you—check out the Corwin list of titles at www.corwinpress.com, and they are there for you to fill in the potholes my awkward paving provides here. So, alas, I feel like I'm abandoning this discourse on the beloved profession you're soon to join. But I do have some final comments.

I tried to have you focus on a continuum of the teaching arc: *getting there*, where you have to prepare your mind and heart for the challenges you will have to respond to creditably and appropriately; *being there*, when you have to speed up your learning curve and discover how little you do know about kids, subject, and self and catch up; and *staying there*, where you must try to buck the eroding factors of exhaustion, frustration, and cynicism to remain vibrant and student-focused, needing to transcend the limitations of higher-ups or know when it's time to move on to another school and group of students.

Here is list of "one more things" before we close about teaching. They echo the title of the recent film *There Will Be Blood* (and I hesitate to tell you that's one of the assured circumstances), because sometimes there will be all sorts of effluvia: blood, barf, or lunch hanging from your face (chicken noodle for me, in the years of the thick moustache). Someday I'll be brave enough to write the five most embarrassing things that happened to me in teaching—all quite amusing. But to close—seven for-sure things that will happen to you as a teacher:

There will be tears. Powerful moments occur in this profession—whether it's a student making a breakthrough revelation, an unburdening of the heart, or just you realizing how limited and fragile we teachers all are, yet when devoted to a common purpose—improving the chance children have to succeed—noble.

There will be failure. You will mess up—little things like forgetting stuff, medium things like not planning well or being nimble enough to recognize a teachable moment as it passes by, and big things that will hurt children or cause anger in parents or consternation from your bosses. We all mess up in all three categories. Driving home beating yourself up mentally for being so lax or blind or cold or knuckleheaded or limited will not be an isolated incident. Learn by negation—learn what not to do ever again, and your prospects improve. That implies you will be constantly reflective about your practice, for in that reflection growth occurs. If you will not or cannot reflect, no amount of preparation will prevent the plethora of errors that will ensue. Those errors will compound upon each other, and you will curl in a ball when the morning alarm blares and hope the day goes away. You know the term used in college by professors, publish or perish? In teaching it's reflect or fail.

There will be triumph. One day you are going to fly your way home because something clicked so well that you understand why you went through all this *sturm und drang* to become a professional educator. If you're lucky, it's a whole classroom thing where everyone gets it, succeeds, laughs in an uproar, and you'll feel like you were born to do this. Most of the successes are quieter and with deeper resonance. When a student gives you that "Oh, I see" look and that out of the panoply of adults who have disappointed, misjudged, or abused, *you* may very well be one of the trustworthy ones, you will understand the responsibility you shoulder.

There will be camaraderie. Unless you land in a school so deeply dysfunctional everyone uses sarcasm as a form of communication, you will find friends in teaching who can help or assuage your gnawing sense of unease as your mistakes pile up. If there is an administrator who senses your inner goodness and worth, you have a treasure because your abilities improve when you sense someone on the power team has your back and knows your value. As previously warned, however, rely on your instincts for there are adults you will meet who are corrosive to your teaching soul.

There will be confusion. You will not know what to do sometimes—sometimes when you must react. Trust your tenets—the why you are there. Advocate for your students and against what gets in the way of their learning. Delay judgment, but doing nothing will be the worse thing you can decide to (not) do.

There will be peace. It does get better and you will get better. No job of extreme importance gets mastered in a year or two. But five years in, you'll have a stronger sense of your teaching self, and by eight years or so, you'll have hit a stride bolstered by experience, reflection, and resolution not to continue or compound failure.

Among the songwriters I deeply admire is Rickie Lee Jones, whose life path has endured both triumph and tragedy, and the honesty of her art and its simple brilliance has always inspired me. One of her breakthrough albums was *The Evening of My Best Day.* The title song relates the horror and humiliation of being bullied. But another voice comes from within the lyric to soothe and point to the better day. I could swear it is a teacher's voice:

Someday, many years from here,

Where no one else can see,

You'll dig up the things they buried

And finally set them free,

Finally, set them free. . . .

And it's a good life

From now on,

When I look back at you.

A good life,

Look ahead—

The sky is almost blue.

There will be many blue skies you will point to for the students you have yet to meet. There will be many blue skies you will create yourself in the minds and hearts of the students you will meet. That's the secret power of teaching done well—the power to help your students see their possibility of a future they but dimly see right now. The other secret power of teaching is while helping your students to see the blue sky to come, you almost inadvertently craft one for yourself.

It's a good life from now on, if you've a mind to working hard and a spirit of reflection and resolution. My words are done. May God be with you as your words as a teacher begin. May they instruct and enlighten, unburden and heal.

There's the bell.

References

Allensworth, E., Correa, M., & Ponisciak, S. (2008). *From high school to the future—Too much too late: Why ACT scores are low in Chicago and what it means for schools.* Chicago: University of Chicago Consortium on Chicago School Research.

Baratz, S., & Baratz, J. (1970). Early childhood intervention: The social science base of institutional racism. *Harvard Educational Review, 40*(1), 29–50.

Bettleheim, B. (1975). *The uses of enchantment: The meaning and importance of fairy tales.* New York: Vintage.

Bradbury, R. (1952). "The sound of thunder." In *A medicine for melancholy.* New York: Doubleday.

Brueghel, P., & Orenstein, N. (1989). *Pieter Brueghel the Elder.* New York: Metropolitan Museum of Art.

Gorski, P. (2006). "Savage Unrealities" *Rethinking Schools Online, 21*(2), http://www.rethinkingschools.org/archive/21_02/sava212.shtml

Guest, J. (1993). *Ordinary people.* New York: Penguin.

Haberman, M. (1995). *Star teachers of children in poverty.* New York: Kappa Delta Pi.

Hayakawa, S. I. (1949). *Language in thought and action.* New York: Harvest. (Original work published 1941)

Hunter, M. (1994). *Enhancing teaching.* New York: Macmillan.

Kant, I. (2008). *Critique of pure reason.* New York: Maugham Press.

Kelly, F., McCain, T., & Jukes, I. (2009). *Teaching the digital generation: No more cookie-cutter high schools.* Thousand Oaks, CA: Corwin.

Kidder, R. (1996). *How good people make tough choices: Resolving the dilemmas of ethical living.* New York: Fireside.

Ladson-Billings, G. (1994). *The dreamkeepers: Successful teachers of African-American children.* San Francisco: Jossey-Bass.

Lazar, A., Pinto, C., & Warren, N. (2006). Perceptions of children's culture in an urban school, *Excelsior 1*(1), 15–28.

National Association of Attorneys General. (1999). *The National Association of Attorneys General School Search Reference Guide of 1999*. Retrieved April 19, 2009, from http://www.doj.state.or.us/hot_topics/doc/naag_campus_safety_task_force_report.doc

Shakespeare, W. (1998). *Othello*. New York: Signet.

Shakespeare, W. (2009). *Hamlet*. New York: Penguin Classics.

Walker, A. (1996). *The color purple*. New York: Pocket Books.

Warren, R. P. (1996). *All the king's men*. New York: Harvest.

Wilder, T. (1998). *Our town*. New York: Harper Perennial.

Wright, B. F. (Illus.). (1992). *The original Mother Goose*. New York: Running Press.

Zipes, J. (Trans.). (1992). *The complete fairy tales of the brothers Grimm*. New York: Bantam.

Index

CORWIN
A SAGE Company

The Corwin logo—a raven striding across an open book—represents the union of courage and learning. Corwin is committed to improving education for all learners by publishing books and other professional development resources for those serving the field of PreK–12 education. By providing practical, hands-on materials, Corwin continues to carry out the promise of its motto: **"Helping Educators Do Their Work Better."**